PASTA AND NOODLES

Merry White received her Ph.D. in sociology from Harvard University in 1980. She is presently lecturer in Harvard's Department of Sociology and head tutor of the East Asian Studies program. Also a professional cook and caterer, she has traveled extensively throughout Europe, the Middle East, and Asia.

Edward Koren is a cartoonist for *The New Yorker* and the illustrator of *Cooking for Crowds*.

Drawings by EDWARD KOREN

PASTA AND NOODLES

Merry White

PENGUIN BOOKS

Penguin Books Ltd, Harmondsworth,
Middlesex, England
Penguin Books, 625 Madison Avenue,
New York, New York 10022, U.S.A.
Penguin Books Australia Ltd, Ringwood,
Victoria, Australia
Penguin Books Canada Limited, 2801 John Street,
Markham, Ontario, Canada L3R 1B4
Penguin Books (N.Z.) Ltd, 182–190 Wairau Road,
Auckland 10, New Zealand

First published in the United States of America
under the title *Noodles Galore* by Basic Books, Inc., 1976
Published in Penguin Books under the title
Pasta and Noodles 1981

LIBRARY OF CONGRESS CATALOGING IN PUBLICATION DATA
White, Merry, 1941–
Pasta and noodles.
Reprint of the 1976 ed. published by Basic Books,
New York under title: Noodles galore.
Includes index.
1. Cookery (Macaroni). 2. Noodles. I. Title.
TX809.M17W48   1981   641.8'22   80-39718
ISBN 0 14 046.504 9

Printed in the United States of America by
Fairfield Graphics, Fairfield, Pennsylvania
Set in Caledonia

For Jenny

Acknowledgments

More people than I can possibly mention here have helped with this book. One who did more than help, however, and whose name should be on the title page, is my husband, Lew Wurgaft, who did the research, testing, eating, and typing for many of the recipes, and who is even now cheerfully planning our next noodle dish.

My parents also deserve more than a line for their support and help, in this as in everything.

However, I especially want to thank those who have so generously given me their recipes, who have gathered up strands of their noodle heritage and presented them to me. Most of these people are mentioned with their specific recipes. Those who are not, including Trin Yarborough, Tom Gold, Leslie Blumberg, Judith Strauch, Beatriz Bloom, Steve Kapos, and Lisa DeFrancis, I thank here.

Farrell Wallerstein, my editor and friend, has been a great encouragement and thoughtful guide. And the prospect of doing this book with Ed Koren has been a constant source of cheer. The drawings are, as ever, a delight.

Contents

Introduction

There is no staple food of human invention as varied and as widespread as the noodle. Noodles appear in virtually every culture, in a dazzling profusion of shapes, and in a surprising variety of cooking styles. While we tend to think first of Italian pasta, we should also note that noodle dishes are a commonplace of Asian cuisine. And they appear elsewhere as well, in such exotic forms as sweet cornstarch noodles served with syrup and rosewater ice cream from India, fiery hot soup noodles from Tibet, and an amazing assortment of "fast-food" noodle snacks from Japan. In the pages that follow I will, of course, draw on the more familiar "mainstream" of noodle cookery, but just as often I will draw on the more esoteric noodle traditions that particularly appeal to me.

The principal reason, of course, for the universality of the noodle is its economy. Traditionally, noodles have served as an alternative staple food in many parts of the world. We in the United States may have a wider choice of foods, but noodles can provide us with a nourishing and inexpensive staple as well. We should, in fact, learn from cultures where economy is a necessity to limit our intake of meat protein. In Asia, for instance, meats, vegetables, and eggs are often used as garnishes for grains and grain products, rather than vice versa. We may not wish to go so far as that. But with a small amount of meat (between one-half and one pound), you can serve six people a filling and nutritious main course. And, as our section on vegetable dishes will show, it is possible to plan interesting and satisfying meatless meals using noodles as a base.

However practical a food the noodle may be, its history is embroidered with romance and mythology. Among the "myths of origin," the most popular one revolves around Marco Polo's trip to the Orient in the 1270s. Among the treasures he brought back with him, the noodle is said to have had the most importance. Yet the existence of the noodle in Italy predated his trip, for rules governing the size and shape of noodles existed there as early as 1200. It is also said that his reports of Chinese noodles used already existing Italian words for these foods, and didn't involve neologisms. And yet the tradition serves a useful symbolic purpose, for it ties together, however apocryphally, the two greatest noodle-making cultures, Italy and China. The issue of who was first (and the Chinese, during an archeological excavation, recently discovered a petrified prehistoric noodle dumpling) belongs as much to the world of "politics" as it does to the history of food.

As we have already suggested, it is hard to find a culture that does not use some form of noodle, whether borrowed long ago and assimilated, or added to the diet recently, in a still self-conscious adaptation. The Chinese "great tradition" spread through Southeast Asia, Japan, and westward through Burma, India and the Middle East where it meets the easternmost fringe of the European noodle. In many Asian societies, rice culture exists side by side with wheat culture, and noodles are often made from rice, soy beans, potatoes, and other substances as much as from wheat.

European noodles take their style from Italy, but also from a later and more robust tradition, the fresh noodles of Middle Europe—as, for instance, German dumplings, Czech spaetzle, and Jewish noodle puddings. Argentine noodle dishes, too, are influenced by the Germans, as well as by the Italians. And, like other aspects of our culture, American noodle dishes are hybrids as well—Chicago chow mein, spaghetti with meat sauce, macaroni and cheese.

All of these cultural crosscurrents stimulate a cook's imagination. Besides tasting good and being economical, noodles are wonderful for their versatility. I often buy the day's nicest, cheapest, most seasonal produce, a bit of meat or fish, and a pound of noodles whose shape has caught my eye. Armed with no recipe but with a knowledge of the properties of the ingredients, I can produce an interesting meal quickly. Noodles are a great liberator, and the recipes in these pages will give you some ideas of how and where to begin.

There is a special magic for me in watching noodles being made. The places themselves are wonderful. An Italian noodle factory, even a small one producing an impoverished sixty varieties out of the possible six hundred now made in Italy, is a combination of traditional lore (what shapes at what seasons, who is entrusted with the old family noodle dough recipe, and so forth) and technical efficiency. After contemplating a small glass case filled with samples of sizes and shapes, you order by pound, shape, and size. Then you watch as an old woman in black feeds a perfectly kneaded and flattened sheet of dough into an enormous contraption, surely a relic of the industrial revolution, and gives the handle five healthy turns to produce a tray of beautiful, floury ribbons of fettucine. Or, if you are lucky, it is the day on which tortellini are made, and she places a pound or two, dusted with cornmeal and flour, lovingly into a box, with rapid-fire directions about cooking them.

Pasta secca (dried noodles) are sold in fascinating varieties in groceries. If you are not bound by the traditions of what pasta to serve with what sauce, then a choice becomes an exercise in whimsy or aesthetic taste. An artist friend bought her husband a birthday gift of about forty varieties of noodles, whose wonderful names—lumache ("snails"), fusilli ("twists"), gemelli ("twins"), farfallette ("little butterflies"), and so on—appeal as much as the shapes.

In some cultures noodles have a sacred as well as a dietary function. Near the town of Pokhara in Nepal I saw brilliantly colored swirls of translucent rice noodles laid out to dry in the sun on deep green banana leaves. As I later learned, they served as both food and offerings to the gods. In other places pasta has been used for purely decorative purposes—dyed, painted, and lacquered into necklaces and pictures. At least the painted Nepali noodles were offerings for gods to *eat*.

NOODLE DEFINITIONS

In writing this book, I have encountered some difficult problems of definition. Just what is a noodle, and what is not? Simply for the purpose of keeping this project manageable, I have decided that any flour paste that is boiled or cooked in liquid and has certain recognized shapes, or categories of shape, is a noodle. Nonetheless, I have included certain "noodles" that don't fit, and left out some which do. For instance, though I have included a few Italian stuffed pasta dishes, I have not included absolutely delicious, comparable Chinese stuffed noodle dough pastries. Such foods as *shiu mai,* "Peking ravioli," bean paste dumplings, and shrimp balls are among my favorite foods, but, like the Italian *tortellini* and *capelletti,* are somewhat difficult to make well. I admit to yielding to lazi-

ness, and, when I can, I prefer to eat them freshly, though professionally, made.

In addition, there is a group of recipes that I enjoy making, but that do not completely fit my "definition" of noodles. These I have called "near noodles," since they are a little more than dumpling, if less than macaroni; these recipes appear later in the book.

NOODLE NUTRITION

Noodles are made of many substances, with varying nutritional worth. Yet even the simplest wheat flour and water noodle has more protein and carbohydrates than potatoes, and, since noodles are often served in sauces containing some combination of vegetable, cheese, or meat, the nutritional balance is very good.

Some years ago, a Maryknoll priest working in Hong Kong invented a recipe that could utilize surplus foods in a very high-protein noodle. He set up a factory producing 7,000 pounds of noodles a day made from 5 per-

cent powdered milk, 20 percent corn meal, and 75 percent wheat flour. This kind of noodle can be made at home, with various high-protein flours, and you can experiment with vegetable additions as well (cooked, and liquidized).

An important nutritional aspect of noodles is their catalytic property in combination with vegetable protein, a phenomenon that has attracted attention recently. Roughly, the idea is that certain starches, such as rice and wheat flour, produce the effect of heightening, "stretching" the protein content of certain vegetable proteins found in legumes such as beans. Thus Mexican rice and beans, and Nepali rice and lentils (*dahl baht*) are nutritionally reasonably well balanced. Thus, too, the perfect noodle meal: *pasta e fagioli*.

Recently, athletes have been encouraged to eat pasta before performing, since it both provides a burst of energy and, unlike sugar "boosters," sustains the energy over a long period of time. Of course, before the Big Game no athlete would devour a large plate of spaghetti and meatballs, but I can imagine eating a cupful of small macaroni, tossed with yogurt, scallions, and freshly ground pepper, and then climbing a small mountain. . . .

These nutritional discoveries seem to invalidate the arguments against pasta put forth in the twenties and thirties by the Italian Futurists, a group of artists and poets who were engaged in revolutionizing every aspect of Italian society. They were especially interested in food and produced a cookbook (*La Cucina Futurista*), which includes a polemic against pasta. In their own way, they were romantics of the machine age, and idolized speed. They wrote "aeropoetry" and made dishes of meat resembling rocket ships.

Thus the ideal men were *"agili, desti, veloci, elettrici,*

furibondi," and their diet had to conform to the new style of life. F. T. Marinetti, often the spokesman for the group, saw a future where food was only the medium for a kinaesthetic experience, and where nutrition came in pill form, taken daily. When eaten, meals were to be light, the inspiration, not the inhibitor of action. Marinetti saw pasta as the enemy of the new, sinewy, heroic warrior-Italian, whose brain would be slowed as well as his body, and whose virility could be greatly threatened, by a dish of spaghetti.

Though pasta may have been the enemy to the Futurists, it is the friend of our present need for a balanced, inexpensive diet. And the Italian varieties of pasta are not the only alternative. The following pages will try to suggest the amazing variety of ways in which noodles are made and cooked throughout the world.

NOODLE TYPES

One of the purposes of this book is to introduce you to the enormous variety of Asian noodle recipes, as well as to the many delicious Western dishes. I'll begin with some basic Asian noodle types, available wherever there is a Chinese or other Asian grocer.

Rice sticks. Chinese and Southeast Asian noodles used stir-fried, soaked, and simmered, but especially deep-fried. When tossed in hot oil, they puff up and increase about six times in volume and become very light and crisp.

Rice chips. Similar to rice sticks, also usually deep-fried. They come in small chips instead of long thin noodles.

Wheat or egg and wheat noodles. These are sold fresh or dry, but are much the best fresh. Chinese egg noodles come both wide and narrow; the wheat noodles are usually flat. Substitute linguine for them if you cannot find them fresh. You can package fresh noodles in plastic and freeze them almost indefinitely, so, once you have a supplier of fresh Chinese noodles, you are well set.

Bean thread noodles. These are both Chinese and Japanese. They are thin, translucent noodles that are used simmered in soups, soaked in hot dishes, and used in *mizutaki* or in Chinese hot-pot dishes. They are made from the mung bean, from which most bean sprouts are made.

Cellophane or vermicelli noodles. These are usually made from seaweed, and are very fine, translucent noodles. They are used as above, particularly in cold dishes.

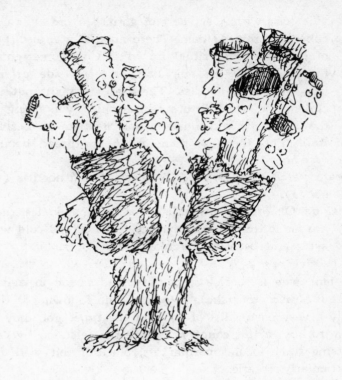

Shrimp noodles. These Southeast Asian noodles are made from shrimp paste mixed with wheat flour. I bought them from one of several Philippine groceries near the Port Authority Bus Terminal in New York, all with wall-to-wall noodles.

Udon. A Japanese wheat noodle, the thickest of Japanese noodles. Used in cold and hot noodle dishes.

Somen. A thinner Japanese wheat vermicelli, used in soups and in cold noodle dishes.

Soba. Made from buckwheat flour, and slightly greenish in color, this is the most popular Japanese noodle. The noodle restaurants that are all over Japan pro-

vide *soba* with every sort of garnish, from eel to ice
cubes and minced ham. These noodles are, also, part
of Japanese social ritual, for when a newcomer enters
his new home the neighbors on each side present
him with *soba* noodles. These are to point out the
closeness of their future relationship by punning on
the word *soba,* which also means "next to" or "beside."

Shirataki. The Japanese name for bean thread noodles
(*see above*).

Potato starch noodles. Used like bean thread noodles (*see
above*).

Phaluda. One of the few indigenous Indian noodles, these
are made from cornstarch paste and served cold with
syrup and rosewater ice cream (*kulfi*) or fruits.

Italian pasta is so rich in variety, and poetic in names,
that it is hard to make a selection. The following is thus
only a very partial list of some of the types you may be
able to buy in this country. I made the selection by can-
vassing three local supermarkets, places I felt were not
particularly esoteric.

One interesting fact is that Italian pasta is divided
roughly into two main varieties, and these have a definite
geographical distribution: northern noodles are flat ribbons
of various widths; southern pasta is tubular.

Whenever possible, where fresh pasta is unavailable,
buy imported Italian pasta.

Lasagne. Wide flat noodles, used layered with vegetables,
meats, and cheese, or sometimes rolled with a filling
and covered with sauce before baking. Parboil before using, as with other large, stuffable pasta like
shells and large tubes.

The following are all interesting shapes of macaroni, or
thicker noodles, usually less than two inches long:

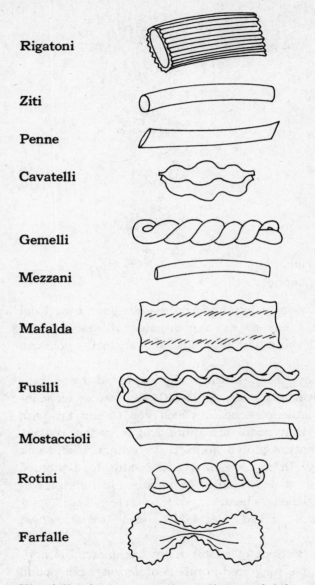

Rigatoni

Ziti

Penne

Cavatelli

Gemelli

Mezzani

Mafalda

Fusilli

Mostaccioli

Rotini

Farfalle

The following are small noodles, useful in soups or buttered in place of rice, or in cheese dishes:

Orzo

Pastina

Acini di pepe

Chili macaroni

Small macaroni

Alphabets
(you can also buy
Hebrew alphabet noodles)

There are obviously hundreds more—do your own local survey—and I haven't even mentioned all the sizes of spaghetti, all the stuffable shells, and so forth, you can find easily.

Noodles have been satisfactorily exploited by a burgeoning health food industry. Health food stores have interesting varieties of noodles, which you should try with the warning that some are quite fragile, when cooked, because of the low-gluten flours they contain. Undercook them slightly. In my neighborhood health food store I counted about a dozen different noodles, including: sesame-rice, artichoke-wheat, soy-rice, whole wheat, spinach-egg, corn, mixed vegetable, and tomato-wheat noodles.

A note on portions of pasta: many commercial American noodles give suggested numbers of servings per pound on the package. Two ounces dry pasta per serving is the size most often given. I find this is quite inadequate, especially for a main-course noodle dish, and recommend one pound of noodles for four to six people, depending on the meal and the other ingredients of the dish. If a simple dish like linguine with *pesto* is being served as a main course, six people would probably require two pounds of linguine. All the recipes in this book are designed for six servings.

HOMEMADE NOODLES: SOME BASIC RECIPES

There are some recipes in this book that specify the use of homemade (or fresh from a factory) noodles. I strongly suggest that you try making them at least *twice*. The first time will seem like work, the second will be more fun and more natural. The product of both will be noodles so delicious they'll seem like a new sort of food altogether. And look for local noodle makers—Italian, Chinese, German, whatever—whose noodles you can buy fresh. You can freeze fresh noodles, in plastic bags, for months.

Although not exhaustive, this section will give you a few basic recipes and instructions for making several types of noodles. Each recipe yields approximately one and a half to two pounds of noodles.

Fresh Pasta

This pasta is made without eggs, takes less rolling, and is easier to work. However, it dries out quickly and must be kept under cloths while it is being used. It can be used both for noodles and for stuffed pasta.

4 tablespoons (½ stick) butter
2 cups unbleached white flour, preferably semolina
2 pinches of salt
Boiling water as needed to make a stiff dough
(usually less than 1 cup)

Put the butter and flour in a mixing bowl and mix them together with your fingers. Add the salt and just enough boiling water to make a stiff dough, then knead until smooth.

Divide the dough into two parts and let it rest under a towel on a board for 30 minutes.

If you are using a pasta machine, proceed as on page 23. If you are making your pasta by hand, roll each half of the dough out, as thin as possible, on a floured board. (Make sure you have a big enough board before you start, or use a clean tabletop.) Turn the dough as you roll it out, and flour it well. For cutting and cooking the pasta, see page 22.

Fresh Egg Pasta

This pasta is good for fettucine and other flat noodles, for *cannelloni*, lasagne, and *tortellini*. Use semolina flour if you can get it—but be sure it's the *flour,* not the fine-grained semolina cereal, which looks like Cream of Wheat.

4 cups unbleached white flour, preferably semolina
1 tablespoon warm water
1 teaspoon salt
3 whole eggs plus 1 egg yolk

Sift the flour onto a large board or tabletop, then make a well in the middle. Combine the water and salt to dissolve the salt, and place in the well with the eggs and the yolk. Gradually mix the flour into the liquids, then knead thoroughly to make a smooth, firm dough. Add more water, if necessary, or, if dough is sticky, knead hard and, if necessary, add more flour. Make into a ball, wrap in a dishcloth, and let stand for at least 1 hour.

Divide the dough into four pieces and roll into balls. On a floured surface, roll out each piece into a very thin circle ($\frac{1}{8}$ to $\frac{1}{16}$ inch thick). Place on clean dishcloths and dry for 45 minutes.

If you are using a pasta machine, proceed as on page 23. If you are making your pasta by hand, proceed as on page 22.

Pasta Verde (Spinach Noodles)

This can also be made with fresh spinach, washed, picked over, and cooked in the water clinging to its leaves until wilted.

2 cups unbleached white flour, preferably semolina
2 eggs
$\frac{1}{2}$ teaspoon salt
8 ounces frozen spinach, thawed, squeezed dry,
and chopped very fine

Combine all the ingredients, then add just enough warm water, bit by bit, to make a firm, elastic dough.

Form the dough into a ball and let it rest on a board for 1 hour, covered with a dishcloth.

If you are using a pasta machine, proceed as on page 23. If you are making your pasta by hand, proceed as on page 22.

Soy Bean Noodles

4 cups soy flour
1 teaspoon salt
2 egg yolks

Combine all the ingredients with enough cold water to make a soft but firm dough. Roll in waxed paper and set aside for 2 hours in the refrigerator.

If you are using a pasta machine, proceed as on page 23. If you are making your own pasta, roll out and cut the dough as described on page 22. Then drop the noodles into boiling salted water for 5 minutes.

MODELING THE NOODLES

By Hand

Prepare the dough according to your recipe. Let it stand for the required amount of time, then:

For regular noodles: Roll out the dough on a floured tabletop or board as thin as you can, turning constantly and adding more flour as needed. Roll the dough up into a jelly roll shape, then flour a sharp knife and cut across into thin coils of noodles, ⅛ inch wide or whatever width you desire. Immediately open up the noodles and dry them on dishtowels or a floured surface, or toss them immediately into boiling, salted water and cook according to the directions on page 24.

For stuffed pasta: Roll out the dough on a floured tabletop or board as thin as you can. Cut with a sharp, floured knife into whatever size noodles are required (rectangles for cannelloni, or lasagne, or whatever) and dry as above before using. Always let noodles dry slightly before stuffing.

By Machine

Prepare the dough according to your recipe and let it stand for 30 minutes to 1 hour, covered. If your machine has not been used before, run a piece of flour-and-water dough through, according to manufacturer's directions, before using. This will remove any dirt or oil in it.

Using the side of the machine for kneading and flattening the dough, run pieces of dough through until you have very flat, regular, rectangular pieces, beginning with a thick dough and gradually adjusting the dial for thinner and thinner pieces. Work slowly so that you don't rip the dough.

Use as is, or cut into rectangles for cannelloni or lasagne or for ravioli. Or put through the cutting side of the machine to form flat noodles, such as fettucine, according to manufacturer's directions. Let the noodles dry as described on page 22 before stuffing or boiling.

COOKING METHODS

I will not be dogmatic about method: I prefer to give you several possible methods that I know work, and let you choose. In any case, noodles vary so much in the amount of time they need, depending on their freshness, their size, the amount of water and size of the pot, that I think the only way of knowing when they are done is to taste constantly after the first 5 or 10 minutes (again, depending on size: the larger ones don't need testing for at least 10 minutes).

Al dente means (and this is vague enough) the stage when the noodle is just firm enough to be firm and springy and not mushy to the tooth, but not so firm that at its core it is hard. You can only learn by trying; it is not a skill learned verbally.

When noodles reach this stage, drain them immediately in a colander and, unless otherwise specified, run cold water over them for a few seconds, tossing them a little. This rinses off starchiness that might make them sticky. It is a good idea to toss freshly cooked pasta with oil (olive, sesame, peanut) or butter immediately after draining, depending on the recipe you are using.

Methods for Cooking Dry Pasta

Large-Kettle Boiling

Bring a 5- to 10-quart kettle two-thirds full of water to a rolling boil. Add 1 tablespoon salt (some add the same of oil). Gradually add the noodles, so as not to stop the boiling, and stir once with a large fork, to separate the noodles. After the first 5 minutes for small or thin noodles, the first 10 minutes for thick ones, begin to taste. When *al dente*, drain quickly in a colander and rinse with cold water. Add oil or butter and toss.

Off-Heat Cooking Method
for Macaroni and Thicker Noodles

Bring a large kettle of water, as above, to a rolling boil and add the noodles all at once. Stir once. Put a tight-fitting lid on the pot, turn the heat off completely, and don't

open for 20 minutes. Drain well and proceed as above. (I prefer the first, since you can test the noodles more easily, but this is a good nonfuss method.)

Three-Step Chinese Method

Bring a large kettle of water to a rolling boil and add the noodles. When they rise to the top, add 1 cup cold water. When it comes to the boil again, add another cup of cold water. When it boils the third time, the noodles should be done (taste). Drain the noodles and let them cool in a basin of cold water, if they are to be used in a cold recipe.

Method for Cooking Fresh Pasta

Bring a large kettle of water to a rolling boil. Add 1 tablespoon salt, then the noodles, and cook for 3 to 5 minutes. Taste for doneness, then drain as above.

Double-Cooked Noodles

1. Boil noodles *al dente* according to any method. Drain well and let dry slightly, spread on a platter. Heat 2 tablespoons peanut or olive oil in a wok or large skillet. Fry the noodles, stirring, until browned.

2. Fry fresh or dry noodles in a heavy skillet, with 2 tablespoons oil as above, *before* boiling. When browned, toss into a pot of boiling water and continue cooking, tasting after 3 minutes for fresh noodles, after 5 minutes for dried. Drain as above.

PURCHASING INGREDIENTS

Pasta

Although U.S.-made noodles are certainly acceptable for most dishes, if you once try imported Italian-made pasta, you probably won't want to switch back. The difference is very great. As mentioned above, always be on the lookout for makers of fresh pasta—it can be frozen.

Exotic Ingredients

Some of the ingredients in this book must be bought from import grocers; each has been marked with an asterisk whenever it appears in a recipe.

The following can be bought at Middle Eastern or Indian grocery stores:

Tamarind
Kashmiri mirsch (a red pepper)
Imported (preferably Madras) curry powder
Ground curry spices, including fenugreek seed
Chick-pea flour

The following can be bought in Chinese grocery stores, as well as in many Japanese:

Soy sauce
Oyster sauce
Chili paste with garlic
Dried shrimp
Dried mushrooms
Fish sauce
Sesame oil
Tiger lily buds ("golden needles")
Wood ear fungus
Fresh ginger
Dried red chilies

Rice flour
Pea flour
Sesame paste
Salted, fermented black beans
Chinese cabbage
Szechuan brown peppercorns
Canned fishballs
Quail eggs (in jars)
Hoisin sauce
Bean paste
Bean curd
Hot chili oil
Noodles, fresh and dried (see pages 19–21)
Barbecue sauce
Chinese sausages
Bamboo shoots
Szechuan preserved vegetables
Snow peas

The following can be bought in Japanese shops (see also the list above):

Miso bean paste
Daikon (long white horseradish)
Rice wine vinegar
Soy sauce (I always get Kikkoman brand)
Aonoriko (dried, pulverized seaweed)
Noodles, fresh and dried (see pages 19–21)
Ramen (packaged noodle instant snack foods)
Sansho pepper
Togarashi (hot red pepper)
Wakame (dried seaweed)
Dashi (Japanese soup stock)
Beni shoga (pickled ginger)
Pickled vegetables
Wasabi (horseradish) powder

GRATING CHEESES

For many of the dishes in this book, and not all of those Italian, the quality of the grating cheese is very important. It doesn't pay to buy pre-grated Parmesan or Romano in a shake-tin; they cost enough anyway, so you may as well spend a little more and get fresh hard cheeses to grate yourself. Buy a little hand cheese grater, or use an ordinary kitchen grater, and it is scarcely more work. And instead of always using Parmesan, try some of the others on this basic list of Italian grating cheeses.

Parmesan—the best of which is labeled *parmigiano reggiano.*
Romano—sharper, saltier than Parmesan. A sheep's milk cheese.
Romano pecorino—a variety of Romano, made from ewe's milk.
Asiago—a nutty taste, made in Wisconsin
Caciocavallo—like an aged provolone
Sardo—similar to Romano pecorino

Soups

Mussel Noodle Soup

Mussels make an elegant first course for a large dinner. This soup is also excellent as a main course—perhaps thickened with a bit more spaghetti, and served with some fresh garlic bread.

½ cup olive oil
2 cloves garlic, finely chopped
2 tablespoons tomato paste
Salt and freshly ground black pepper to taste
1 teaspoon oregano
1 tablespoon finely chopped fresh basil, or 1 teaspoon dried
5 cups water
3 dozen mussels in shells, scrubbed well and beards scraped off
8 ounces thin spaghetti
½ cup chopped fresh parsley

Heat the oil in a large saucepan. Add the garlic and brown lightly, then add the tomato paste, salt and pepper, oregano, basil, and the 5 cups of water. Bring to a simmer, then add the mussels. Cover and let simmer for about 10 minutes (when all the mussels are open, the soup will be done).

Meanwhile, boil the thin spaghetti *al dente* (see page 24). Drain well, place in tureen, and pour the mussels and broth over. Serve, garnished with the parsley.

Fishball Soup

This is a very convenient sort of soup, since most of the ingredients can be in your larder if you live near a Chinese grocer. Fish balls are very delicate, unfishy and easily overwhelmed by stronger flavors—they are rather like delicate *quenelles*—so if you use the pungent, fresh coriander, use it lightly.

6 cups chicken broth
Salt and pepper to taste
1½ tablespoons soy sauce *
⅔ cup soaked, shredded dried bean curd skin *
5 dried mushrooms,* soaked and sliced, soaking
water reserved
1 can Chinese fishballs *
1 package (2 ounces) vermicelli or Chinese bean
thread *
2 teaspoons sesame oil *
2 tablespoons chopped scallions and fresh
coriander or parsley

Put the broth on to heat and season with salt, pepper, and soy sauce. Add the bean curd skin and the mushrooms and their liquid, and bring to a simmer. Add the drained fishballs and vermicelli or Chinese bean thread and simmer for 5 minutes.

Just before serving, add the sesame oil, scallions, and coriander.

Clam Broth with Mushrooms and Small Shells

A more delicate concoction than traditional chowders, but reminiscent of the New England variety. A good main-dish soup, served with salad and crusty bread.

1 can (10 ounces) small clams
1 medium onion, finely chopped
4 tablespoons (½ stick) butter
¼ pound fresh mushrooms, sliced
3 egg yolks
½ cup milk
Salt and freshly ground black pepper to taste
1 tablespoon cornstarch dissolved in 2 tablespoons
warm water
1 cup chicken broth
½ cup small shells
1 tablespoon chives

Sauté the onion in 2 tablespoons of the butter until soft. Add the mushrooms and sauté over high heat for a few minutes, then set aside.

Place the egg yolks in a soup tureen and beat them lightly with a fork while gradually adding the milk. Then add the remaining butter, which has been mashed until soft and creamy.

In a separate pot add a cup of water to the chicken broth and bring to a boil. Add the small shells and boil for a few minutes. Then slowly mix in the dissolved cornstarch, and add the clams in their juices and the mushrooms.

Pour the hot soup very slowly into the egg-yolk mixture, beating rapidly with a whisk as you pour, until all the soup has been added. Top with chopped chives and serve.

Hot and Sour Noodle Soup

Hot and Sour soup must now be the most popular Chinese restaurant soup, preempting wonton soup. This version with shrimp noodles is very rich and filling, and will certainly do as a main-course soup.

¼ cup tiger lily buds ("golden needles") *
¼ cup dried mushrooms *
¼ cup wood ear fungus *
3 tablespoons dried shrimp *
6 cups chicken broth
2 tablespoons soy sauce *
Salt and Tabasco to taste
1 package dried shrimp noodles * or 1 cup
broken-up thin egg vermicelli
1 teaspoon sesame oil *
Red wine vinegar to taste
1 tablespoon cornstarch dissolved in 1 tablespoon
cold water
2 eggs, beaten lightly
3 scallions, shredded

Put the tiger lily buds, dried mushrooms, wood ear fungus, and dried shrimp into small, separate bowls. Cover with hot water and let soak for 20 minutes, then drain. Shred the tiger lily buds, mushrooms, and wood ear fungus.

Bring the broth to a boil in heavy kettle. Add the soaked ingredients, soy sauce, and salt and Tabasco to taste. Lower the heat, add the noodles, and simmer until the noodles are cooked.

Just before serving, stir in the sesame oil, vinegar to taste, the cornstarch mixture, and the eggs, and stir for 1 minute while simmering. When thick, garnish with the scallions and serve, along with extra vinegar and Tabasco.

Grandmother's Chicken Noodle Soup

This is the old favorite, but even heartier than the soup grandmother used to make. Now it can be the centerpiece of a dinner instead of just an appetizer. And the chicken that is left over will make a nice salad for another meal.

1 small chicken, left whole
3 stalks celery, including leaves, cleaned and
chopped
1 medium onion
3 carrots, scraped and chopped
4 sprigs fresh parsley
1 large pinch dried thyme
1 bay leaf
6 peppercorns
Salt and freshly ground pepper to taste
2 tablespoons finely chopped fresh parsley
4 ounces thin, flat egg noodles

Place the chicken in a large, heavy saucepan and add water to cover. Bring slowly to a boil, removing the scum as it floats to the top. When no more scum rises, let simmer and add the celery, onion, carrots, parsley, thyme, bay leaf, and peppercorns. Keep at a low simmer, partially covered, for 2 or 3 hours, adding water as needed to keep the chicken covered.

Remove the chicken and set aside. Strain the soup well, discarding the soup vegetables. Pull the chicken meat from the bones and dice, reserving 2 cups of the chicken for the soup and setting the rest aside for another purpose.

Return the soup to the kettle, along with salt and pepper to taste, the finally chopped parsley, the chicken meat, and the egg noodles. Simmer until the noodles are tender, then serve.

Japanese Clear Chicken Soup with Vermicelli

It is said that a Japanese cook is judged by the clarity of his soup—it should be crystal clear and scarcely colored. You should be able to gaze into the depths of the bowl and see the carefully arranged garnishes. Sometimes there may be a shred of black mushroom and a tiny pink shrimp, or a strip of lean pork and a crisp, bright green peapod. The garnishes provide aesthetic interest and contrasts in color and texture. In this recipe, form the translucent noodles into a swirl suggesting a nest and add one sprig of cress and one strip of seaweed to the bits of chicken. Understatement is the key.

1 chicken breast (for a yield of 1/4 pound meat)
3 cups water
3 cups canned chicken broth
1 teaspoon salt
Sansho pepper * to taste
3 ounces thin rice noodles or bean thread,* soaked
in warm water
6 small strips *wakame* (Japanese seaweed),*
soaked in warm water
Watercress

Place the chicken breast, water, and broth in a saucepan and bring slowly to a boil. As the gray scum rises to the surface, carefully skim it off with a large spoon. When the broth begins to boil, immediately lower the heat to a bare simmer. Let the broth simmer for 1 hour, partially covered, then strain well and set aside. Let the chicken breast cool.

When the chicken breast is cool, remove the skin and

bones, then pull and cut the meat into neat shreds. Sprinkle them with salt and *sansho* pepper.

In separate serving bowls, place a swirl of noodles, chicken shreds, strips of *wakame*, and sprigs of watercress. Heat the broth just to a simmer and carefully pour over the ingredients arranged in the bowls.

Mandalay Coconut Khawksway

Lorna Chin of Boston's Mandalay Restaurant let me watch her in the kitchen making this and other wonderful Burmese dishes. The rich garlicky broth, smooth coconut milk, and crisp fried noodles make one of the best soups I've had. For a few weeks when we first discovered Mrs. Chin, we had this dish at least once a week, at her place or ours.

½ cup peanut oil
1½ cups finely chopped onion
8 cloves garlic, peeled and sliced
2 tablespoons minced fresh ginger *
2 fresh green chilies, seeded and finely chopped
2 dried red chilies, mashed in a mortar
1 tablespoon turmeric *
2 teaspoons salt
2 tablespoons rice or pea flour *
1 tablespoon paprika
6 cups water
3 pounds chicken pieces, cut up into small pieces,
across the bones
1 pound thin egg noodles
3 cups Coconut "Milk" (see below)
½ cup chopped scallions
1 cup crunchy fried noodles (store-bought, or
see note below)
Lemon wedges

Heat the oil in heavy saucepan. Add the onion, garlic, and ginger and sauté until lightly browned. Add the fresh chilies, then lower the heat and let simmer into a paste, stirring occasionally. It will take four or five minutes.

Add the dried chilies, turmeric, salt, rice flour, and paprika and stir-fry for 3 minutes over medium heat. Add the water and bring to a boil; then lower the heat to a simmer. Add the chicken pieces, cover, and let simmer for 40 minutes.

Remove the chicken pieces and set aside. Continue to simmer the soup, uncovered, for 2 to 3 hours.

Boil the egg noodles in salted water *al dente* (see page 24), then drain and place in a serving dish. Taste the broth for seasoning, then add the coconut "milk" and heat to a simmer. Add the chicken pieces, heat through, and pour both chicken and soup over the noodles. Garnish with the scallions, fried noodles, and lemon wedges.

Note: Instead of buying fried noodles, you can cut up cooked linguine and deep-fry it until golden. Drain it well before you use it.

Coconut "Milk"

Let 2 cups unsweetened coconut shreds, or grated fresh coconut, sit in 3 cups hot water for 1 hour. Pour into a clean cloth held over a bowl and squeeze the liquid through the cloth. Pour the liquid through the coconut again, and you will have 3 cups of "milk."

Ham and Bean Thread Soup

This soup is an original combination of appealing Asian tastes. But don't hesitate to serve it as the first course of a Western meal. One caution: be sure to separate the bean threads as you place them in the broth. Once I didn't and had a very hard time getting them apart as they cooked.

1 bag *dashi* *
4 cups boiling water
5 dried mushrooms,* soaked in warm water for
20 minutes, soaking water reserved
3 thick slices smoked ham
1 tablespoon soy sauce *
1 teaspoon sesame oil *
Salt to taste
2 ounces bean thread *
2 scallions, chopped

Place the *dashi* bag in the boiling water and simmer for
20 minutes.

Squeeze the mushrooms dry, then slice and add to the
broth, along with the water they soaked in. Slice the ham
into shreds and add to the simmering broth, along with
the soy sauce, sesame oil, and salt to taste.

Boil the bean thread in 1 quart of water until soft—
about 5 minutes—then drain, separating the noodles as
you add them to the broth. Add the chopped scallions just
before serving.

Vietnamese Pho (Beef Soup)

Pho is a very popular Vietnamese soup that is often a
main dish. The amount of fish sauce can be adjusted. It
is a peculiar taste at first, and needs some getting used to.
If you can't find it, try using half the quantity of anchovy
paste.

2 pounds beef shin
3 medium onions, finely chopped
2 tablespoons finely minced ginger *
¼ teaspoon ground fennel seeds
1 teaspoon salt
2 packages (2 ounces each) vermicelli (Italian)
or Homemade Noodles (see below)
1 tablespoon vinegar
2 tablespoons fish sauce *
Chopped scallions and shredded fresh green chilies
for garnish

Place the beef in a 3-quart saucepan and cover with water. Bring to a boil, skimming, then reduce the heat and
simmer for 3 hours, or until tender. Remove the beef and
cool.

Meanwhile, add the onions, ginger, fennel seeds, and
salt to the broth and simmer for 15 minutes. Add the
vermicelli or fresh noodles and simmer for 8 minutes
longer, then add the vinegar, fish sauce, and the meat,
removed from the bones and shredded. Garnish with scallions and chilies and serve.

Homemade Noodles

1 cup all-purpose flour
1 egg
¼ cup water

Combine all the ingredients and knead until smooth.
Force the dough through a ricer into the boiling soup.

Soupe à la Ahmed

A fairly unusual noodle/vegetable soup, quite sufficient for a supper with crusty bread and salad. This North African mixture reminds me a bit of Ukranian borscht and a little of minestrone. The lemon at the end is quite essential.

¼ pound margarine or ½ cup olive oil
3 medium onions, sliced thin
3 cloves garlic, minced
3 large carrots, scraped and sliced
1 large potato, peeled and diced
⅓ head red cabbage, thinly sliced
1 large can (36 ounce size) Italian plum tomatoes
½ can (6 ounce size) tomato paste
1 cup diced celery
2 small zucchini, diced
½ pound lean boneless lamb, shredded
½ teaspoon each dried rosemary, thyme, basil,
and cayenne pepper
3 quarts water
3 or 4 swirls of thin egg noodles (about 3 cups
cooked)
½ cup orzo (rice-shaped noodles)
3 tablespoons chopped fresh parsley
Lemon wedges

Heat the oil or margarine in a very large, heavy kettle, then add the onions and garlic and sauté until golden. Add all the other ingredients except the pastas, parsley, and lemon wedges. Bring to a boil, then reduce the heat and simmer for 45 minutes.

Add the egg noodles and orzo and cook for 10 minutes longer, then serve, garnished with the parsley and accompanied by lemon wedges.

Passatelli in Brodo

This soup could scarcely be simpler. A greatly comforting dish, a midnight snack, a prelude to a heavier meal, a convalescent treat. These *passatelli* are halfway between a dumpling and a noodle—a little firmer than the Roman *stracciatella,* which is closer to an egg-drop soup, and less firm than spaetzle.

6 cups beef or chicken broth
Salt and freshly ground pepper to taste
1 bay leaf
½ teaspoon thyme
5 eggs
5 tablespoons freshly grated Parmesan cheese
5 tablespoons dry bread crumbs
White pepper

Put the broth into a large saucepan. Season with the salt, pepper, bay leaf, and thyme, then bring to a boil.

Meanwhile, combine the eggs, Parmesan, bread crumbs, and salt and white pepper to taste in a small saucepan. Heat, stirring to blend, only a minute or so, then, holding a ricer, spaetzle maker, or sieve over the broth, which should now be boiling, press the paste into the broth. Let simmer a few minutes, then serve with more grated Parmesan.

Pasta in Brodo with Stracciatella

Like *passatelli*, this soup is a comfort. The tiny "pepper-corn" pasta provides interesting texture and contrast to the wisps of cheesy egg-drop. *Stracciatella* is one of the most common Roman preludes to a meal.

5 tablespoons acini de pepe ("peppercorn" soup pasta)
6 cups chicken broth
3 eggs
3 tablespoons freshly grated Parmesan cheese
Salt and freshly ground black pepper to taste

Boil the acini de pepe for 6 minutes, then drain.

Heat the chicken broth in a kettle. While it is getting hot, combine the eggs and Parmesan in a mixing bowl, beating with a fork. Add the noodles to the broth and simmer gently for 1 minute, then, using a fork, stir the soup rapidly in a circular motion to set up a whirlpool. Dribble the egg mixture in, as the soup swirls around, to form shreds; in a minute or so, the egg will set. Serve immediately, with salt and pepper to taste.

Broccoli Soup with Spinach Noodles

This is a new twist on a favorite Roman soup, which blends the flavors of prosciutto and broccoli. And the spinach noodles make it doubly green. Be sure to drain off most of the salt pork fat or the broth will be too greasy for most palates.

2 tablespoons olive oil
2 cloves garlic, minced
2 onions, minced
4 slices prosciutto, diced
Freshly ground black pepper to taste
1 bunch broccoli, separated into florets
¼ pound salt pork, diced
2 tablespoons butter
3 cups chicken broth
1 cup green spinach noodles, broken into small
pieces
¼ cup freshly grated Parmesan cheese

Heat the olive oil in a large pot, then sauté the garlic, onion, and prosciutto until soft. Add the pepper and enough water to cover and simmer, covered, for about 20 minutes.

In another pot, cover the broccoli florets with water and cook until tender but still crisp.

In a saucepan sauté the salt pork in the butter until crisp, then drain off most of the fat. Place the drained broccoli in the pan with the salt pork and simmer for 5 minutes, then add to the prosciutto mixture, making sure it is well blended. Stir in the chicken broth and bring to a simmer.

Meanwhile, cook the pasta *al dente,* (see page 24). Drain and add to the soup, then serve, topping each portion with the Parmesan cheese.

Minestrone Milanese

This is a delicious variation on a classic Italian soup. Take special care in cooking the vegetables added at the end. If they retain some of their crisp texture, the soup is fresher tasting.

3 medium onions, finely chopped
3 carrots, scraped and finely chopped
2 parsnips, scraped and finely chopped
3 cloves garlic, finely chopped
3 chicken or beef bouillon cubes
3 tablespoons butter or oil
Salt and freshly ground black pepper to taste
1 bay leaf
4 cups water
1 large can (35 ounce size) tomatoes, drained
and roughly chopped
1½ cups cooked or canned white beans
3 medium zucchini, sliced
½ cup pastina or orzo (rice-shaped noodles)
½ cup fresh or frozen peas
2 tablespoons chopped fresh parsley

In a large, heavy saucepan, sauté the onion, carrots, parsnips, and garlic in the butter or oil until tender. Add the bouillon, salt, pepper, bay leaf, and water. Bring to a boil, then reduce the heat and simmer for 30 minutes. Add the tomatoes and simmer for 30 minutes longer. (The soup can be set aside at this point.)

One-half hour before serving, add the beans and zucchini and bring to a simmer. Add the noodles and peas and cook just until the noodles are tender. Serve garnished with parsley, and pass crusty garlic bread and freshly grated Romano cheese.

Summer Minestrone

Minestrone is certainly not a hot weather soup, which is a shame, since summer is when all the vegetables are at their best. This version, though most of the traditional ingredients are missing, still leaves you with a refreshing summer shadow of the heavier minestrones.

1 tablespoon olive oil
1 small onion, finely chopped
2 cloves garlic, finely chopped
4 medium tomatoes, peeled, seeded, and finely chopped (see page 51)
5 cups chicken broth
½ cup vermicelli, broken in small bits
2 small zucchini, thinly sliced
1 green pepper, finely chopped
Salt and freshly ground black pepper to taste
2 tablespoons chopped fresh parsley

Heat the olive oil in a large, heavy saucepan. Add the onion and sauté until golden, then add the garlic and stir for 1 minute. Add the tomatoes and chicken broth and bring to a boil. Cook for 15 minutes, then add the vermicelli and zucchini and cook for 5 minutes, or until the vermicelli is tender. Add the green pepper and remove from the heat. Chill.

To serve, add salt and freshly ground black pepper to taste and garnish with parsley.

Mexican Vermicelli Soup

One unusual aspect of this recipe is the sautéing of the noodles before they are cooked in the soup, which gives them a pleasant, nutty taste; the method can be tried in other noodle recipes. This is quite a straightforward soup, which gains in sophistication when the sherry is added.

2 tablespoons olive oil
2 ounces vermicelli or fine egg noodles
1 onion, chopped
1 clove garlic, finely chopped
4 medium tomatoes, peeled, seeded, and chopped
(see note below)
2 quarts beef stock (not bouillon)
Salt and freshly ground black pepper to taste
Pinch of granulated sugar
1 tablespoon chopped fresh parsley
¼ cup dry sherry

Heat the oil in a heavy saucepan. Sauté the uncooked noodles until golden brown, then drain and set aside.

Put the onion, garlic, and tomato in the blender and blend until uniform but not liquefied. Cook this mixture in the oil remaining in the pan for 5 minutes, stirring constantly. Add the noodles, stock, and seasoning, then cover and simmer until the noodles are tender.

Add the parsley and sherry and serve, with freshly grated Parmesan cheese on the side.

Note: Peel the tomatoes by putting them into boiling water for 20 seconds or so and draining; the skin should peel off easily. Cut in half and squeeze gently over sink or bowl in order to remove the seeds.

Eggs and Cheese

Broad Noodles and Three Cheeses

Sharp Cheddar is important in this robust dish, a very simple variant of macaroni and cheese.

1 cup tomato puree
Salt and freshly ground black pepper
2 teaspoons chopped fresh basil or 1 teaspoon dried
1 pound broad egg noodles
8 ounces sharp Cheddar cheese, finely chopped
4 ounces farmer or pot cheese
½ cup freshly grated Romano pecorino

Preheat the oven to 350 degrees.

Season the tomato puree with salt, pepper, and the basil, then pour into a greased casserole.

Boil the noodles *al dente* (see page 24), then toss with the Cheddar and season with salt and pepper. Put in the casserole and top with the farmer cheese, well crumbled, and the Romano pecorino. Bake for 30 minutes, or until lightly browned.

Macaronatha

Feta gives noodles a sharp and memorable flavor. Once you have added the butter, the faster you can serve this dish the better it will taste. You should be eating it just as the feta softens, and before the noodles have settled into a mass.

1 pound fresh noodles (see pages 19–21)
1 cup crumbled feta cheese
¼ pound (1 stick) sweet butter

Boil the noodles *al dente* (see page 24), then drain well and place in a serving bowl. Sprinkle the cheese over the noodles and mix well.

Melt the butter in a heavy saucepan, and when it is just beginning to brown, pour it quickly over the noodles. Toss lightly and serve at once.

Noodles with Kephalotiri Cheese and Browned Butter

Kephalotiri is a cheese difficult to find if you don't live in an area that has Greek groceries. Search a little. Although I haven't tried it myself, I hear that it freezes well, so if you do find some, get extra and put it aside for the future.

Browned butter with noodles is quite delicious, as are slightly burned noodles; you could also sauté the cooked noodles in butter until both are browned.

1 pound thin spaghetti
5 tablespoons butter
8 ounces *kephalotiri* cheese, crumbled
Salt and freshly ground black pepper to taste

Boil the thin spaghetti *al dente* (see page 24). Drain well, then put in a serving bowl.

Heat butter carefully in a heavy skillet. Let it get to a deep brown, but don't let it burn. Toss the thin spaghetti with the kephalotiri and brown butter and add salt and plenty of pepper. Serve at once.

Macaroni and Cheese

Macaroni and cheese is an old standby, but it is surprising how much a little attention to detail can improve what would ordinarily be just another meal. For instance, buttering the casserole well and coating with bread crumbs produces the crust people fight over.

8 ounces elbow macaroni
2 tablespoons butter
2 tablespoons all-purpose flour
2 cups milk, scalded
2 cups medium sharp Cheddar or longhorn cheese, roughly grated
1 teaspoon salt
Freshly ground black pepper to taste
Dash each of Tabasco and Worcestershire sauce
½ cup bread crumbs
¼ cup freshly grated Parmesan cheese

Preheat the oven to 325 degrees.

Boil the macaroni *al dente* to a *firm* stage (see page 24).

Meanwhile, heat the butter in a saucepan. Stir in the flour and let bubble for 1 minute, then add the milk, whisking as you do so to prevent lumps. Let simmer as the mixture thickens, then stir in the Cheddar until it is melted. Add, off the heat, the salt, pepper, Tabasco, and Worcestershire sauce.

Combine the bread crumbs and Parmesan cheese. Butter a small casserole well and coat with ¼ cup of the bread crumb mixture. Drain the macaroni and toss with the sauce. Pour into the casserole, top with the remaining bread crumb mixture, and bake in the preheated oven for 45 minutes to 1 hour, until crusty brown.

Farmer's Noodles

Like several other cheesy noodle dishes, but perhaps lighter and fresher tasting, for the noodles are tossed with the cheese instead of being baked into it. Do not neglect to add sugar and something crisp and green—peas, as suggested below, or perhaps finely shredded green peppers, or strips of fresh fennel.

1 ½ pounds egg noodles
2 tablespoons butter or margarine
8 ounces farmer, pot, or cottage cheese
½ cup chopped scallions
½ cup peas, cooked only 4 or 5 minutes, until *just* tender, or another green vegetable
1 teaspoon granulated sugar
Salt and freshly ground black pepper to taste

Boil the noodles until *al dente* (see page 24). Drain and place in a bowl; add the butter or margarine and toss well. Add the cheese, tossing with a fork, then toss with the scallions and the peas or other vegetable. Season to taste with the sugar, salt, and pepper and serve immediately.

Spaghetti Tossed with Cheese

What a simple dish! Yet the mingling of different cheeses produces a subtle flavor often lacking in more complicated recipes. Naturally, you may want to experiment with your own combinations of cheeses.

1 ½ pounds spaghetti
½ cup freshly grated Gruyère cheese
½ cup freshly grated Parmesan cheese
½ cup freshly grated Fontina cheese
½ cup melted butter
Salt and freshly ground black pepper to taste

Cook the spaghetti *al dente*, (see page 24), then drain well and place in a large warmed bowl. Toss with the cheeses, pouring the hot butter over all. Toss again, adding salt and pepper, and serve at once.

Spaghetti with Yogurt Sauce

A recipe that shows just how quickly it's possible to assemble a noodle dish both interesting in flavor and inexpensive. For a heavier dish, you can substitute ricotta for the yogurt.

1 pound spaghetti
1 tablespoon butter
2 tablespoons olive oil
1 small onion, finely chopped
3 cloves garlic, finely chopped
3 tablespoons tomato paste
Salt and freshly ground black pepper to taste
1 ¼ cups plain yogurt

Cook the spaghetti *al dente* (see page 24), then drain and toss with the butter. Set aside and keep warm.

Heat the oil in heavy skillet. Add the onion and garlic and sauté until golden, then stir in the tomato paste. Season with salt and pepper.

Turn off the heat and stir in the yogurt. Toss with the spaghetti and serve.

Noodles Romanoff

This is an especially rich combination of noodles, sour cream, and cheese that will satisfy a large crowd of people. It can be frozen for weeks, or refrigerated a few days before baking. Very suitable for a buffet supper.

2 packages (8 ounces each) fine noodles
2 packages (8 ounces each) cream cheese, softened
1 pint commercial sour cream
¼ cup minced onion
1 teaspoon Worcestershire sauce
½ teaspoon garlic salt
Dash of Tabasco
1 teaspoon salt
½ cup buttered bread crumbs

Preheat the oven to 350 degrees.

Cook the noodles *al dente* (see page 24), then drain and place in a large bowl.

Combine the cream cheese, sour cream, onion, and seasonings, stirring well to mix, then stir into the cooked noodles. Pour into a greased 2-quart casserole, top with the bread crumbs, and bake for about 25 minutes.

Omelette aux Nouilles

Omelets can be vehicles for many leftovers, and noodles work well in this one. Besides mushrooms, you might also add chopped vegetables—spinach, green beans, broccoli —almost anything will do.

2 tablespoons herbs (fresh chives, parsley, thyme, tarragon, in whatever mixture you like)
8 eggs
1 teaspoon salt
Freshly ground black pepper to taste
1½ cups cooked thin noodles
3 tablespoons butter
½ cup mushrooms, sliced and sautéed in 4 tablespoons butter

Combine the fresh herbs, eggs, salt, pepper, and noodles.

Heat butter in large skillet until bubbly, then pour in the egg/noodle mixture and cook, without stirring, over medium heat until the edges and bottom are set. Sprinkle the mushrooms over the top, then, using a spatula, fold one side over the other. Remove from the pan and serve.

Note: If you prefer to serve the omelet unfolded, cover it and let cook until set.

Cheese Noodle Soufflé

A soufflé seems like an odd place to find a noodle, yet the contrast is delicious, and the dish is like an aerated, delicate macaroni and cheese.

8 ounces macaroni or noodles, cooked *al dente*, drained well
5 eggs, separated
1½ cups White Sauce (page 267)
Salt and freshly ground black pepper to taste
Freshly grated nutmeg to taste
1 cup freshly grated Gruyère cheese
¼ cup freshly grated Parmesan cheese

Preheat the oven to 400 degrees.

Cook the noodles *al dente* (see page 24), then drain well and place in a well-buttered casserole.

Add the egg yolks, one by one, to the white sauce, beating well. Season with salt, pepper, and nutmeg and stir in the Gruyère. Fold in the egg whites, stiffly beaten.

Top the noodles with the egg mixture, sprinkle with the Parmesan, and bake in the preheated over for 45 minutes, or until puffed and brown.

Macaroni Georgina

A nice, quick luncheon dish. The eggs should be soft boiled, and shelled carefully. The centers should run when cut into.

6 eggs
1 pound small macaroni
2 cloves garlic, finely minced
3 tablespoons softened butter
½ pound fresh mushrooms, sliced and sautéed in 2 tablespoons butter until soft
Salt and freshly ground black pepper to taste

Boil the eggs for 5 minutes, or long enough to set the whites but leaving the yolks soft. Shell them carefully and set aside, covered to keep warm.

Boil the macaroni *al dente* (see page 24), then drain. Sauté the garlic in butter until golden. Toss the macaroni in the garlic butter, then add the mushrooms and salt and pepper and toss lightly.

Serve with the eggs in the center of a "nest" of noodles.

Cottage Cheese and Sour Cream Noodle Pudding

This is a relative of the great family of Jewish noodle puddings, which are usually sweet. When I sent out a call for noodle puddings, I must have received thirty variations on the sweet sort, and only two for savory cheese. This is an adaptation of one by Clara Gilman.

1 ½ pounds curly egg noodles
¼ pound (1 stick) butter or margarine
1 cup sour cream
1 ½ cups cottage cheese
2 eggs
3 scallions, finely chopped
½ teaspoon dillweed or 2 tablespoons finely
chopped fresh dill
Salt and freshly ground black pepper to taste

Preheat the oven to 350 degrees.

Boil the noodles for 5 minutes, then drain and toss with the butter first, then the remaining ingredients. Place in a buttered casserole and bake for 1 hour, or until browned.

Cannelloni with Spinach and Feta Filling

Well worth the effort. Homemade pasta squares for this dish make all the differences, but the filling can be used in bought shells or manicotti, boiled *al dente* (see page 24)

before stuffing. In either case, you can assemble the whole thing ahead of time, to be frozen or refrigerated before baking.

**1 package spinach (10 ounces), washed and
picked over
2 onions, finely chopped
2 cloves garlic, finely chopped
2 tablespoons butter
4 ounces feta cheese, crumbled
4 ounces farmer cheese, crumbled
Pinch of freshly grated nutmeg
Salt and freshly ground black pepper to taste
2 eggs
¼ cup chopped fresh parsley
Fresh Egg Pasta (page 19)
3 cups Fresh Tomato Sauce (page 264)**

Sauté the onion and garlic in the butter in a deep saucepan until golden. Remove from the heat and stir in the spinach and the two cheeses. Beat in the seasonings, eggs, and parsley, then refrigerate while you prepare the pasta dough.

Roll the dough out as thin as possible and cut it into 3 × 5-inch rectangles. Let these dry on clean dishtowels for at least 1 hour, then cook them for 3 to 5 minutes in a large kettle of boiling, salted water. Drain and place on dishtowels.

Butter a 9 × 13 × 2-inch baking dish. Place about 2 table-spoons of the filling on each rectangle and roll up. Place side by side, seam side down, in the baking dish. Pour tomato sauce over all. (At this point, you may refrigerate or freeze.)

Preheat the oven to 350 degrees. Bake the cannelloni for 30 minutes, or until bubbly. Serve immediately, with freshly grated Parmesan cheese on the side.

Macaroni, Spinach, and Cheese

Here is another pleasant change from the usual macaroni and cheese. You might try other parboiled or sautéed vegetables, like eggplant or Swiss chard.

4 tablespoons (½ stick) butter
¼ cup all-purpose flour
2 cups milk
1 teaspoon salt
Freshly ground black pepper and nutmeg to taste
1 package (10 ounces) spinach, washed and picked over
8 ounces sharp Cheddar cheese, shredded
2 cups cooked macaroni
¼ cup bread crumbs

Preheat the oven to 350 degrees.

In a saucepan, heat butter until it melts. Add the flour and whisk, then add the milk gradually, while beating, and bring to a simmer, stirring as the sauce thickens. Add the salt, pepper, and nutmeg and simmer for 3 minutes.

Meanwhile, cook the spinach in the water remaining on the leaves until wilted, then drain well.

Stir in all but 2 tablespoons of the cheese into the sauce and remove from the heat. In a buttered baking dish, layer the macaroni, spinach, and cheese sauce. Sprinkle with the bread crumbs and remaining 2 tablespoons of cheese and bake for 45 minutes, or until bubbly and browned.

Odamaki-mushi
(Japanese Noodle Custard)

A variant on *chawan-mushi,* a savory custard, *odamaki-mushi* includes noodles and other bits hidden in the steamed egg base. You may add shrimp instead of chicken, canned gingko nuts, or small cubes of *tofu* (bean curd), fresh snow peas, or a few fresh or frozen green peas to each cup.

**1 whole chicken breast, raw, boned and cut into ½-inch cubes
1 package (2 ounces) bean thread noodles (*shirataki*),* soaked in warm water for 15 minutes and drained
¼ cup peas, snow peas, bean curd, chopped scallion or whatever contrasting taste/texture elements you choose
1 teaspoon soy sauce *
Salt and *sansho* pepper * to taste
6 medium eggs
2¾ cups broth or *dashi* *
Pickled ginger (*beni shoga*) * for garnish**

In each of 6 small custard cups or heatproof bowls, place a few cubes of chicken and a small swirl of noodles. Add a bit of whatever other ingredients you choose, then sprinkle with ½ teaspoon of the soy sauce, salt, and *sansho* pepper and set aside.

In mixing bowl, beat the eggs well. Add the broth or *dashi,* ½ teaspoon salt, and ½ teaspoon soy sauce, then divide the mixture between the cups. Cover each cup with foil.

If you have a large steamer, use it. If not, place a rack

(a preserving rack will do) or upside-down plate in a large kettle. Place the cups on the rack and add boiling water carefully up to the bottom of the cups, but not touching them. Cover the pot and steam over moderate heat for 10 to 15 minutes, or until the custard is firm. Serve lukewarm, garnished with the pickled ginger.

Vegetables

Pesto Genovese
(Frank Phillips' Version)

Pesto is a real treat, even more so because to make it I must denude half my crop of carefully tended basil—but it is worth it. Some who love it are tempted to make it in the basil-less winter by using dried basil in combination with parsley. Don't. Use freshly grated Romano and pignoli, if you can find them. Covered tightly, it keeps for a week to ten days in the refrigerator, and can be used on cold shrimp or boiled chicken as well.

½ cup chopped fresh parsley
½ cup chopped fresh basil leaves
4 cloves garlic, chopped
⅓ cup pignoli (pine nuts)
½ cup freshly grated Romano cheese
Salt and freshly ground black pepper to taste
Italian olive oil as needed (approximately one cup)
2 pounds linguine

In the container of a blender place the parsley and basil, about half at a time of each. To each batch add half the garlic, pignoli, cheese, and salt and pepper to taste, and then add the olive oil gradually, blending until smooth.

Boil the linguine *al dente* (see page 24). Drain and toss with the *pesto* sauce, then serve, with extra freshly grated Romano on the side.

Roman Spaghetti

Tossing cooked spaghetti in a flavored oil until browned before adding the tomato sauce gives this dish a certain depth of character. Using a Chinese wok and stir-frying helps to brown it quickly.

1 ½ pounds spaghetti
½ cup olive oil
1 cup chopped onion
1 clove garlic, minced
1 tablespoon fresh basil or 1 ½ teaspoons dried
3 cups Fresh Tomato Sauce (see page 264)

Boil the spaghetti *al dente* (see page 24), then drain very well.

Heat the oil in a heavy skillet or wok. Add the onion and garlic and sauté until golden, then add the basil. Add the spaghetti and toss over high heat until well mixed, browned, and heated through, then toss with the tomato sauce.

Serve immediately, with freshly grated Romano cheese on the side.

Broccoli and Anchovy Sauce with Small Shells

Broccoli and anchovies, both strong tastes, do not war with each other in this combination. Keep the broccoli *al dente*—undercooked—for preference. When it is over-done, its color changes to a sort of army olive and it has a sickly taste and texture.

1 medium head broccoli, cut into small florets
2 tablespoons olive oil
1 can (2 ounces) anchovy fillets, chopped
3 tablespoons butter
Salt and freshly ground black pepper to taste
½ pound small macaroni shells
6 tablespoons freshly grated Parmesan or Romano
cheese

Cook the broccoli in boiling water until just tender, about 5 minutes, then drain and set aside.

Place the oil in a frying pan over medium heat and add the chopped anchovies. Mash the anchovies into a paste with a wooden spoon, then sauté the broccoli in the anchovy sauce for about 5 minutes, adding 2 tablespoons of the butter to thicken the sauce. Add salt and pepper to taste.

Meanwhile, boil the shells *al dente* (see page 24), drain them, and mix with the remaining butter and grated cheese. Then pour the broccoli and anchovy sauce over the shells and serve.

Fettucine alla Romana

A classic combination of peas, prosciutto, and freshly made pasta. The trick is to have everything done at once, and to toss it all together just before eating. One often sees this dish assembled in a chafing dish at table.

1 pound fresh fettucine, homemade (see pages 19–21) or factory purchased
6 tablespoons softened butter
1 cup freshly grated Romano cheese
½ cup heavy cream, heated (*not* boiled)
1 cup fresh peas, parboiled
4 ounces prosciutto, finely shredded
Salt and freshly ground black pepper to taste

Boil the fettucine *al dente* (see page 24). Place the butter in a serving dish, then drain the fettucine in a colander and add to the butter. Add the cheese, cream, peas, and prosciutto and toss well. Serve immediately with salt and pepper to taste.

Mixed Vegetables with Pasta

A variant on the mixed vegetable sauce, this time with bacon and a little wine. Very hearty.

4 slices bacon
¼ cup olive oil
½ cup chopped fresh parsley
6 scallions, chopped
2 cloves garlic, minced

1 medium red onion, minced
2 tablespoons chopped fresh basil or 1 tablespoon
dried
½ small head cabbage, shredded
½ pound zucchini, scrubbed and diced
½ pound tomatoes, peeled, seeded, and chopped
(see page 51)
2 green peppers, seeded and diced
1 cup chicken broth
1 tablespoon dry vermouth
Salt and freshly ground pepper to taste
1 pound fresh fettucine, homemade (see pages
19–21) or factory bought, or spaghetti
2 tablespoons butter
Freshly grated Parmesan cheese

In a large, heavy saucepan, sauté the bacon until crisp.
Add the oil, parsley, scallions, garlic, and onion and sauté
for 3 minutes, then add the basil, cabbage, zucchini,
tomatoes, green peppers, chicken broth, vermouth, and
salt and pepper to taste. Simmer, uncovered, for 10
minutes.

Cook the pasta *al dente* (see page 24), then drain and
toss first with the butter, then with the vegetable mixture.
Serve immediately, with freshly grated Parmesan cheese
on the side.

Penne all'Arrabiata

"Angry pasta" is the translation of the above. "Angry"
with hot red chilies, I suppose. This is a very delicious and
fiery dish.

2 tablespoons butter
2 cloves garlic, finely chopped
5 tomatoes, peeled, seeded, and chopped (see page 51)
3 fresh red hot peppers, seeded and finely chopped
1 tablespoon finely chopped fresh basil or 1 ½ teaspoons dried
Salt and freshly ground black pepper to taste
1 pound penne ("quill" noodles)
¼ cup freshly grated Romano pecorino cheese
¼ cup freshly grated Parmesan cheese

Heat the butter in heavy saucepan. Add the garlic and sauté until golden, then add the tomatoes, hot red peppers, basil, salt, and pepper and simmer until the sauce thickens.

Cook the penne *al dente* (see page 24), then drain well. Toss with the cheeses and the sauce and serve.

Pasta con Piselli

This is a filling dish that makes a full meal with a plain green salad and garlic bread. The combination of salt pork and peas in this is very rich.

3 tablespoons cubed salt pork
1 medium onion, finely chopped
2 cloves garlic, finely chopped
1 cup fresh, chopped tomatoes
Salt and freshly ground black pepper to taste
1 teaspoon finely chopped fresh basil or ½ teaspoon dried
1 pound fresh peas, shelled
8 ounces thin spaghetti

Cook the pork in a heavy casserole until browned. Remove the browned bits with a slotted spoon and reserve; leave the fat in the casserole. Add the onion and garlic to the casserole and cook until wilted, then add the tomatoes, salt, pepper, and basil and simmer for 10 minutes.

Meanwhile, parboil the peas in salted water for 5 to 8 minutes, or just until tender. Drain and add to the sauce.

Boil the thin spaghetti *al dente* (see page 24). Drain well, then toss with the sauce and salt pork bits and serve, with freshly grated Parmesan cheese on the side.

Rigatoni with Zucchini

Zucchini, properly cooked, which is *under*cooked, is delicious tossed with noodles. Use lots of freshly ground black pepper.

2 pounds small zucchini
1 teaspoon salt
1 pound rigatoni, cooked *al dente* and drained
2 tablespoons butter
2 tablespoons olive oil
2 cloves garlic, finely minced
2 teaspoons finely chopped fresh thyme or 1
teaspoon dried
Freshly ground black pepper to taste

Scrub the zucchini well and cut into thin strips the size of matchsticks. Salt and set aside for 1 hour, then drain and dry on paper towels.

Cook the rigatoni *al dente* (see page 24), then drain well.

In a large skillet, heat the butter and oil until bubbling. Add the zucchini and sauté, stirring, for 2 minutes. Add the garlic and thyme and sauté for 1 minute longer.

Add pepper to the sauce, then toss with rigatoni and serve immediately with freshly grated Parmesan cheese.

Fettucine with Peas and Mushrooms

Fettucine in peas and cream with prosciutto is a wonderful if common dish; but with peas and the pungent dried mushrooms and nutty fresh ones, a classic dish has a pleasant twist.

2 tablespoons olive oil
3 tablespoons butter
1 pound fresh mushrooms, sliced
1 ounce dried Italian mushrooms, soaked in warm water for 20 minutes, soaking water reserved (see note below)
2 cloves garlic, finely minced
2 pounds fresh fettucine, homemade (see pages 19–21) or factory bought
2 egg yolks
1 cup heavy cream
1 cup fresh peas, parboiled
Salt and freshly ground black pepper
½ cup freshly grated Parmesan cheese
2 tablespoons chopped fresh parsley

Heat the oil and 2 tablespoons of the butter in a large skillet. Add the fresh mushrooms and stir over medium heat until the mushrooms start to exude their juices. Lower the heat, add the garlic, and simmer for 5 minutes.

Squeeze the soaked mushrooms dry, then slice and add to the skillet. Stir for 2 minutes, then set aside.

Boil the fettucine *al dente* (see page 24), then drain. Place in a warm serving dish and toss with the remaining 1 tablespoon butter.

Add the egg yolks and cream to the mushrooms, stirring, then add the peas and stir over *very* low heat until the mixture begins to thicken. Season with salt and pepper.

Toss the noodles and mushroom mixture lightly, together with the Parmesan cheese. Garnish with the parsley and serve at once.

Note: You can freeze the mushroom soaking liquid in a small plastic jar and use it for other sauces.

Spaghetti Ticino

Noodles tossed in cream, with various bits of bright vegetables and prosciutto, are very attractive and easy to prepare. If you can use freshly made pasta, it is much better; the dried pasta seems better with heavier sauces.

5 tablespoons butter
2 tablespoons olive oil
½ pound fresh mushrooms, sliced
3 scallions, finely minced
2 cloves garlic, finely minced
Salt and freshly ground pepper to taste
1 cup diced prosciutto
1½ cups medium cream
1 pound fresh fettucine, homemade (see pages 19–21) or factory bought, or spaghetti
½ cup roughly chopped watercress
½ cup freshly grated Parmesan cheese

Heat 4 tablespoons of the butter and 1 tablespoon of the oil in a heavy skillet, and sauté the mushrooms, stirring, over medium high heat for 3 minutes.

Add scallions and garlic and stir-fry for 2 or 3 minutes more, then remove from the heat.

In a small skillet, heat the remaining butter and oil. Add the prosciutto and cook over low heat. Add salt and pepper.

Add the cream to the mushroom mixture and return to the heat. Cook rapidly, to reduce the liquid, for 5 minutes.

Meanwhile, boil the pasta *al dente* (see page 24), then drain. Add to the mushroom mixture, along with the watercress, then turn off the heat and toss with the prosciutto. Sprinkle with the cheese and serve immediately.

Pasta with Vegetables

Baked pasta dishes (*in forno*) are the only ones Italians consider main dishes. This is a baked version of *ratatouille* with pasta, and it can be frozen or refrigerated before baking.

4 tablespoons (½ stick) butter
2 tablespoons olive oil
2 medium onions, chopped
2 cloves garlic, finely chopped
1 tablespoon chopped fresh oregano or 1 teaspoon dried
1 tablespoon chopped fresh basil or 1 teaspoon dried
Salt and freshly ground black pepper to taste

**4 tomatoes, peeled, seeded, and roughly chopped
(see page 51)
4 small zucchini, scrubbed and sliced
½ cup chicken broth, or more as needed
1 pound small shells or elbows
½ cup freshly grated Parmesan cheese**

Preheat the oven to 350 degrees.

Heat 2 tablespoons of the butter and the oil in a heavy saucepan. Add the onion and garlic and sauté until golden, then add the oregano, basil, salt and pepper, tomatoes, zucchini, and chicken broth and simmer for 5 minutes, or until the zucchini is *just* tender.

Boil the pasta *al dente* (see page 24) and drain well. Toss with the vegetable mixture and place in a large, buttered casserole. Sprinkle the Parmesan over all, dot with the remaining 2 tablespoons butter and bake for 30 minutes, or until golden.

Spaghetti with Uncooked Basil and Tomato Sauce

One of my happiest noodle experiences was the discovery of the mixture of freshly cooked hot pasta with an uncooked vegetable sauce. Very summery and refreshing.

**4 medium tomatoes, peeled, seeded and chopped
(see page 51)
1 pound mozzarella, diced
¼ cup chopped fresh basil
2 cloves garlic, finely minced
1 cup olive oil
Salt and freshly ground black pepper to taste
1 pound spaghetti**

Combine the tomatoes, mozzarella, basil, garlic, oil, salt, and pepper and set aside for 1 hour.

Boil the spaghetti *al dente* (see page 24), then drain and toss with the tomato mixture. Serve immediately, with freshly grated Parmesan cheese on the side.

Pasta with Peppers

Garlicky peppers and tomatoes tossed with hot pasta and served with lemon—another example of an uncooked sauce for hot noodles. In this, as in other simple "raw" sauces, the quality of the ingredients is an important factor. Ripe but not mushy tomatoes, *fresh* basil, and freshly grated cheese are essential.

6 medium tomatoes, sliced very thin
2 sweet red or yellow peppers, seeded and sliced
into thin strips
½ cup roughly chopped fresh basil
3 cloves garlic, finely chopped
Olive oil as needed—at least ¼ cup
Salt and freshly ground black pepper to taste
Freshly grated Parmesan or Romano pecorino
cheese to taste
1 pound rigatoni or similar pasta
Lemon wedges for garnish

Combine the tomatoes, peppers, basil, garlic, oil, salt, and pepper and set aside.

Boil the pasta *al dente* (see page 24), then drain well, shaking. Toss with cheese to taste, more salt and pepper as needed, and the tomato mixture and serve with lemon wedges and more cheese.

Pasta with Dried and Fresh Mushrooms

These dried mushrooms are terribly expensive ($24.00 per pound at last purchase), but luckily an ounce or two goes a long way. In this recipe you soak the mushrooms in warm water. When you drain them for use in the recipe, be sure to save the liquid (I put it in small plastic jars and freeze it, and use it in other sauces).

**2 ounces dried Italian mushrooms, soaked in warm
water for 20 minutes, soaking liquid reserved
1 pound fresh mushrooms, sliced
5 scallions, chopped
½ cup olive oil
2 pimientos, in thin shreds
2 cloves garlic, minced
Salt and freshly ground black pepper to taste
1 pound ziti or rigatoni**

Squeeze the soaked mushrooms dry, then slice and combine with all the other ingredients except the pasta. Set aside for 30 minutes to marinate.

Boil the pasta *al dente* (see page 24), then drain well and toss with the mushroom mixture. Serve immediately.

Shells with White Kidney Beans and Chick-peas

A nice white and red combination, this is similar to *pasta e fagioli* in nutritional value. Although, for simplicity's sake, I here give instructions for canned chick-peas and kidney beans, I prefer dried (soaked overnight and boiled just until tender) because the canned variety tend to be too mushy.

1 pound small shell macaroni
2 tablespoons olive oil
1 large onion, chopped
2 cloves garlic, finely chopped
1 tablespoon chopped fresh basil or 1 teaspoon dried
1 teaspoon dried oregano
½ teaspoon dried thyme
1 bay leaf
Salt and freshly ground black pepper to taste
1 large can (20 ounce size) tomato puree
1 can (20 ounce size) chick-peas
1 can (20 ounce size) cannellini (white kidney beans)
1 pound small shells

Boil the shells *al dente* (see page 24), then drain well.

Heat the oil in a saucepan. Sauté the onion and garlic in the oil until golden, then add the herbs, salt, pepper and tomato puree and simmer for 15 minutes. Add the chick-peas and cannellini and simmer for 15 minutes more.

Toss the sauce with the drained shells and serve immediately, with freshly grated Parmesan cheese on the side.

Vermicelli with Mushroom Sauce

A very quick sauce in which mushrooms, anchovies, and, surprisingly, mint combine deliciously. (Mint is, after all, a cousin to basil.)

2 tablespoons olive oil
3 cloves garlic, finely chopped
1 can (2 ounces) anchovies, drained and chopped
½ pound fresh mushrooms, sliced
1 large can (35 ounce size) tomatoes, drained
and chopped
½ teaspoon chopped fresh mint or ¼ teaspoon dried
1 teaspoon salt
½ teaspoon freshly ground black pepper
1 pound vermicelli

Heat the oil in a skillet, then add the garlic, anchovies, mushrooms, tomatoes, mint, salt, and pepper. Cook for 10 minutes over a medium high flame, stirring frequently.

Meanwhile, boil the vermicelli *al dente* (see page 24). Drain, put into a serving dish, and pour the sauce over. Serve immediately.

Spinach and Noodles in Cream

In my opinion, spinach is best after it has absorbed three times its weight in butter, a rather extravagant French method of dealing with it, or cooked very quickly in olive oil and garlic, a basic Sicilian practice. It also has a natural affinity for cream, and tossed with fettucine is quite delicious.

1 pound fresh spinach, cleaned (with tough stems
removed) and chopped
2 cloves garlic, finely minced
1 small onion, finely minced
3 tablespoons olive oil
2 tablespoons butter
1 pound spinach fettucine
1 cup heavy cream
Salt and freshly ground black pepper to taste

In a large, heavy kettle, sauté the garlic and onion in the oil and 1 tablespoon of the butter until golden. Put in the spinach, cover tightly, and let cook over low heat until just wilted.

Meanwhile, boil the fettucine *al dente* (see page 24). Drain and toss with the remaining tablespoon butter, then toss with the spinach and the heavy cream in the kettle. Heat the noodles through, then season with salt and pepper and serve, with freshly grated Parmesan cheese on the side.

Pasta alla Caponata

Caponata, which this recipe resembles, is a cold eggplant mixture often served in antipasto courses. It is best made ahead, as is this delicious pasta sauce.

2 cloves garlic, finely minced
¼ cup olive oil
1 sweet red pepper, diced
1 sweet green pepper, diced
1 ½ pounds eggplant, peeled and cubed
¼ cup chopped black olives
8 tomatoes, peeled, seeded, and chopped (see page 51)
½ can (2 ounce size) anchovies, chopped
1 tablespoon chopped fresh basil or 1 teaspoon dried
1 teaspoon capers
Salt and freshly ground black pepper to taste
1 pound spaghetti or other pasta

Sauté the garlic in the olive oil for 3 minutes, then add the peppers, eggplant, and olives and simmer for 15 minutes. Add the tomatoes, anchovies, basil, and capers and simmer for 15 minutes longer, then add salt and pepper to taste.

Cook the pasta *al dente* (see page 24). Drain, put into a serving dish, and pour the sauce over. Serve immediately, with freshly grated Parmesan cheese on the side.

Baked Eggplant with Pasta

A layered pasta version of eggplant *parmigiana*. Before baking, this dish can be covered with foil and frozen. It is excellent for large crowds.

2 medium eggplants, peeled and sliced
2 tablespoons salt
½ cup or more olive oil or olive and corn oils, mixed
2 cloves garlic, finely chopped
3 cups peeled, seeded, and chopped tomatoes (see page 51)
2 teaspoons chopped fresh basil or 1 teaspoon dried
Freshly ground pepper to taste
1 pound medium macaroni, boiled *al dente* (see page 24) and drained
½ pound mozzarella, sliced thin
½ cup freshly grated Parmesan cheese

Preheat the oven to 325 degrees.

Toss the eggplant slices in the salt and set in a colander to drain for 30 minutes.

Heat the oil in a large skillet and brown the eggplant slices, a few at a time, adding more oil as needed and removing the eggplant to a plate as done.

Add 2 tablespoons of oil to the skillet and sauté the

garlic until golden. Add the tomatoes and basil and simmer for 15 minutes, adding water if necessary to make a medium thick sauce.

In a buttered casserole, layer the macaroni, eggplant, and tomatoes and top with the cheeses. Bake in a 325-degree oven for 30 minutes, or until the cheeses brown.

Pasta Marinara

Marinara sauce is really a basic tomato sauce with (preferably) fresh herbs. Traditionally it is said to be the simple tomato sauce in which fishermen (hence "marinara") would cook seafood on board their boats. It is best made just before using.

**4 cups canned Italian plum tomatoes, drained
and roughly chopped, or 4 cups peeled, seeded, and
chopped fresh tomatoes (see page 51)
3 tablespoons olive oil
4 medium onions, finely chopped
2 cloves garlic, finely minced
Salt and freshly ground black pepper to taste
1 tablespoon chopped fresh oregano or 1 teaspoon
dried
1 tablespoon chopped fresh basil or 1 teaspoon
dried
1 bay leaf
1 pound spaghetti or any medium pasta**

Put the tomatoes, canned or fresh, through a food mill and set aside.

Heat the oil in a heavy saucepan and sauté the onion until golden, stirring occasionally. Add the garlic and sauté for 2 minutes more, then add the tomatoes, salt, pepper, and herbs and simmer for 30 minutes, partially covered.

Boil the pasta *al dente* (see page 24). Drain well, put into a serving bowl, and serve with the sauce and freshly grated Parmesan cheese on the side.

Spinach Sformato with Pasta

A *sformato* is a baked egg dish, usually with vegetables. This one uses the combination of bacon and spinach.

4 tablespoons (½ stick) butter
1 medium onion, finely chopped
3 pounds spinach, washed and cooked rapidly in the water clinging to the leaves
Salt and freshly ground pepper to taste
4 strips bacon, fried and crumbled
3 tablespoons freshly grated Parmesan cheese
1 tablespoon all-purpose flour
1 cup milk, heated
3 eggs
1 cup cooked macaroni

Preheat the oven to 350 degrees.

Heat 2 tablespoons of the butter in a heavy skillet and sauté the onion until golden. Add the spinach, finely chopped, then season with salt and pepper and add the bacon and Parmesan.

In a separate pan, heat the remaining 2 tablespoons butter and add the flour, stirring well. Add the milk very slowly, whisking to keep the sauce smooth as it thickens. Let cool a little, then add the egg yolks, one at a time, and salt and pepper to taste. Add this béchamel sauce and the cooked macaroni to the vegetable mixture.

Beat the egg whites until stiff and fold gently into the vegetables. Place in a buttered soufflé dish or casserole and bake until bubbly and brown, about 1 hour. Serve with broiled foods, or on its own with a mushroom sauce.

Tortellini with Spinach and Ricotta Filling

Tortellini are to some the height of *pasta ripieni,* or stuffed pasta. The Bolognese call them "navels of Venus," and there are many stories concerning their origin. One has an enamoured cook molding the pasta to fit his lover's navel, in another the inventor has a vision of Venus, and copies her navel. . . . No matter whose navel inspired them, they are delicious—best, I think, tossed in heated heavy cream and Parmesan.

1 package (10 ounces) fresh spinach, washed and picked over
4 tablespoons (½ stick) butter or margarine
3 medium onions, finely chopped
6 slices prosciutto, finely chopped
2 cups ricotta cheese
½ cup freshly grated Romano or Parmesan cheese
Freshly grated nutmeg, salt, and freshly ground black pepper to taste
Fresh Egg Pasta (pages 19–21) made and set aside under a dishcloth while preparing the filling
1 cup heavy cream
Freshly grated Parmesan cheese to taste

Place the spinach in a kettle, with water still clinging to the leaves, and cover tightly. Cook over medium heat just until wilted, then drain in a colander, pressing to remove all the water. Chop fine and set aside.

Heat the butter or margarine in a heavy skillet. Add
the onion and cook, stirring occasionally, until golden.
Add the prosciutto and spinach and cook, stirring, for a few
minutes. Add the ricotta, Romano or Parmesan, nutmeg,
salt, and pepper.

Cut the dough into four portions. Using one at a time
(cover the others), roll out to a thickness of about ⅛
inch. (If the dough is too springy, let it rest longer.) Cut
out circles with a glass about 2 inches in diameter or a
round cutter.

Place a small amount of filling in the center of each
circle, then fold over in a half-moon shape and pinch the
edges tightly together. Draw the ends across the center
and pinch together in a ring.

As you make them, place them, not touching, on a clean
dishtowel and cover. Let them dry out a little for an hour
or so. (The dough must be worked before it dries out,
however, so work quickly.) Repeat with the other three
portions of dough.

At serving time, bring a large kettle to boiling and boil
the *tortellini* for about 5 minutes, or until done (try one).
Drain and keep warm in a serving dish.

Meanwhile, heat the heavy cream carefully with Parmesan to taste and a little salt and pepper. Pour over the
tortellini, toss, and serve at once.

Pasta e Fagioli I

Pasta e fagioli, like some other grain and vegetable combinations (the Nepali rice and lentil curry, for instance) provides a good protein-rich meal, for the protein of the beans is augmented by the catalytic action of the pasta. Anyway, the dish is delicious.

1 beef shank (about 2 pounds)
1 pound small California pea beans or other small
white beans, soaked overnight and drained
2 tablespoons olive oil
3 cloves garlic, minced
1 tablespoon chopped fresh basil or 1 teaspoon
dried
Salt and freshly ground black pepper to taste
5 medium tomatoes, peeled, seeded, and chopped
(see page 51)
1 tablespoon tomato paste
1 pound small macaroni
2 tablespoons chopped fresh parsley
Freshly grated Parmesan cheese

Place the beef shank in a large kettle and add the drained beans. Cover with cold water and simmer, skimming off the scum, until the beans are tender. Remove from the heat.

In a skillet, heat the oil and sauté the garlic until brown. Add the basil, salt, pepper, tomatoes, and tomato paste and cook gently for 5 minutes. Add to the beans.

Cook macaroni *al dente* (see page 24); drain and add to the beans. Pour out the extra liquid and save the beef shank for another dish. Simmer for 5 minutes to heat through, then serve, topped with the parsley and Parmesan.

Pasta e Fagioli II

Of course, the variations on this classic dish are endless. This one is made with dry lentils, so it requires more cooking time, since they aren't presoaked, but long simmering makes them absorb flavors well.

4 slices bacon
2 onions, roughly chopped
2 cloves garlic, finely minced
1 carrot, scraped and chopped
1 green pepper, seeded and chopped
1 can (15 ounces) tomatoes, drained and roughly chopped
4 cups water, more if necessary
2 cups dried red or brown lentils
2 bay leaves
2 teaspoons dried thyme
1 tablespoon dried oregano
1 tablespoon dried basil
1 pound thin spaghetti

In a large, heavy kettle, sauté the bacon. When crisp, add the onions, garlic, carrots, and green pepper. When the onions are golden, add the tomatoes and water and bring to a boil. Reduce to a simmer, then add the lentils gradually, stirring constantly. Add the herbs and simmer for 1 hour or more, until the lentils are tender.

Add the thin spaghetti and more water, if necessary. Cook for 8 minutes more, or until the spaghetti is cooked *al dente*. Serve in bowls, with a side dish of freshly grated Parmesan cheese.

Pasta with Peperonata

Sweet peppers add color and texture, as well as flavor to a tomato sauce. Take special care not to overcook them and lose their texture and fresh taste in the process.

1 tablespoon olive oil
2 tablespoons butter
1 medium onion, roughly chopped
4 sweet red peppers, seeded and cut in thin strips
1 green pepper, seeded and cut in strips
2 cloves garlic, finely chopped
6 large ripe tomatoes, peeled, seeded, and roughly
chopped (see page 51)
12 ounces ziti or rigatoni

Heat the oil and butter in a saucepan and sauté the onion until lightly browned. Add the peppers, cover the pan, and simmer for 10 minutes over low heat, then add the garlic and tomatoes and simmer, covered, for another 30 minutes. (If the mixture is too liquid, simmer with the cover off.)

Boil the pasta *al dente* (see page 24), then drain well. Toss with the *peperonata* and serve, with freshly grated Parmesan cheese on the side.

Spaghetti Zaccharia

This is named after the best six-year-old spaghetti eater I know, Zachary Bell, whose favorite is *pesto,* but it was already taken. The sauce is also called "tomato *piccante.*"

2 tablespoons olive oil
3 large sweet red peppers, seeded and chopped
3 medium tomatoes, peeled, seeded and chopped
(see page 51)
3 cloves garlic, finely minced
1 tin (2 ounces) anchovies, chopped
1 tablespoon capers
Salt and freshly ground black pepper to taste
Lemon juice to taste
1 pound linguine

Heat the olive oil in a skillet. Sauté the peppers briefly, then add the tomatoes, garlic, anchovies, capers, and salt and pepper. Simmer for 5 minutes.

Boil the linguine *al dente* (see page 24) and drain well. Add the lemon juice to the sauce, toss with the linguine, and serve immediately, with freshly grated Romano cheese on the side.

Fettucine con Aspergi

Freshly cooked asparagus, tossed in cream and lightly seasoned, is a delicious accompaniment to fresh noodles.

4 tablespoons (½ stick) butter
2 cloves garlic, mashed
1 pound asparagus, stems peeled, cut in 1-
inch pieces
1 cup heavy cream
1 pound fettucine, preferably fresh, either
homemade (see pages 19–21) or factory bought
Salt and freshly ground black pepper to taste
½ cup freshly grated Parmesan cheese

Heat the butter in a heavy skillet. Stir-fry the garlic in the butter until golden, then add the asparagus and heavy cream and simmer gently, just until the asparagus is tender.

Boil the fettucine *al dente* (see page 24) and drain well. Season the asparagus with salt and pepper and toss with the fettucine, then serve sprinkled with the Parmesan.

Gemelli Milanese

I'm very fond of these gemelli ("the twins"), for they hold onto the sauce well. It is interesting to see that these and other more recondite macaroni forms like scungilli are becoming more common.

4 strips bacon
1 small onion, finely chopped
½ pound fresh mushrooms, sliced
2 cups canned Italian plum tomatoes, roughly
chopped
4 green peppers, seeded and chopped
Salt and freshly ground black pepper to taste
1 teaspoon dry mustard
1 pound gemelli (twisted macaroni)

In a heavy skillet, sauté the bacon. Drain off the extra fat, leaving 2 tablespoons. Add the onion and sauté until golden, then add the mushrooms and sauté until wilted. Add the tomatoes, peppers, salt, pepper, and mustard and cook for 15 minutes.

Boil the gemelli *al dente* (see page 24), then drain and toss with the vegetable mixture. Serve at once, with freshly grated Romano cheese on the side.

Curried Cauliflower with Raisins and Noodles

An unusual combination, but surprisingly delicious. I think of it as a barebones curry without the heat, but with the interesting counterpoints of sweet (raisins) and sour (lime juice), crunchiness (sesame seeds) and smoothness (cauliflower).

2 medium onions, sliced
3 tablespoons mustard oil or peanut oil
1 teaspoon sesame seeds
2 teaspoons cumin
2 teaspoons finely chopped fresh ginger *
1 cauliflower, cut into florets
¼ cup raisins
1½ cups chicken stock
1 tablespoon lime juice
1 teaspoon granulated sugar
Salt to taste
1 pound vermicelli

Sauté the sliced onions in 2 tablespoons of the oil until soft. Add the sesame seeds, cumin, and ginger and sauté for a few more minutes. Add the cauliflower and raisins, then pour in the chicken stock, cover, and simmer for about 10 minutes, until just tender. Add the lime juice, sugar, and salt to taste.

Meanwhile, boil the vermicelli *al dente* (see page 24) and drain. Heat the remaining tablespoon of oil in a wok, add the vermicelli, and stir-fry over high heat for 5 minutes. Top the noodles with the cauliflower mixture and serve.

Mee Rebus

Bean sprouts and hot "curry" ingredients make this Malaysian noodle dish a meeting place of the Chinese and Indian noodle traditions.

8 dried red chilies *
5 scallions, finely chopped
2 tablespoons finely chopped fresh ginger *
1 tablespoon ground coriander
1 teaspoon ground anise
1 teaspoon ground cumin
½ teaspoon ground turmeric
3 tablespoons mustard oil or peanut oil
1 beef or chicken bouillon cube
2 cups water
2 medium potatoes, boiled, peeled, and mashed
1 pound thin egg noodles
3 cups bean sprouts
½ cup dry-roasted peanuts

Grind or pound the chilies, scallions, and ginger together. Combine with the coriander, anise, cumin, and turmeric and set aside.

Heat the oil in a heavy skillet until it smokes. Add the bouillon cube and water and simmer for 2 minutes. Stir in the mashed potatoes.

Boil the noodles *al dente* (see page 24), then drain and place in a serving dish. Add the bean sprouts, sauce, and peanuts, and toss well before serving.

Szechuan Noodles (Vegetable Version)

This version of Szechuan noodles combines bean sprouts, spinach, and noodles in a typically spicy cold sauce that includes sesame paste or peanut butter. A similar Szechuan dish with chicken is also included (see page 216).

1 pound fresh Chinese egg noodles * or fresh Soy Bean Noodles (see page 21)
2 tablespoons peanut oil
3 tablespoons soy sauce*
1 tablespoon vinegar
2 teaspoons chili paste with garlic * or Tabasco to taste mixed with 2 cloves minced garlic
2 tablespoons sesame paste,* *tahini,* or peanut butter
1 tablespoon sesame oil *
½ cup chicken broth
½ pound fresh bean sprouts, washed and picked over
6 ounces fresh spinach, roughly chopped

Parboil the fresh noodles for 5 minutes, or soy bean noodles less, *al dente.* Drain well.

In a large wok, heat the peanut oil. Toss the noodles in the oil until they are heated through and beginning to brown.

Combine the soy sauce, vinegar, chili paste with garlic, sesame paste, sesame oil, and broth. Place all sauce ingredients in a serving bowl and mix well. Add the noodles, bean sprouts, and spinach and toss well. Serve immediately.

Curried Vegetables with Egg Vermicelli

Many Indian dishes, though not originally served with noodles, do very well with them. This is a colorful vegetable curry.

2 medium onions, finely chopped
2 tablespoons mustard oil or peanut oil
1 tablespoon minced fresh ginger *
1 tablespoon minced garlic
1 teaspoon whole fenugreek seed *
2 teaspoons turmeric, ground
1 teaspoon coriander, ground
1 teaspoon cumin, ground
1 teaspoon hot paprika or *kashmiri mirch* *
1 teaspoon salt
½ teaspoon pounded dried red chilies *
¼ teaspoon ground cinnamon
5 zucchini, scrubbed and sliced
1 small eggplant, peeled and cubed
1 green pepper, seeded and sliced
3 medium tomatoes, peeled, seeded, and chopped
(see page 51)
1 carrot, scraped and sliced
1 tablespoon peanut oil
1 pound egg vermicelli, fresh Chinese * or dried

Sauté the onion in the oil in a large skillet. Add the ginger, garlic, all the spices, and the salt and sauté until the garlic is soft, about 5 minutes. Add all the vegetables and cook, covered, until soft, about 30 minutes.

Parboil fresh noodles for about 5 minutes or cook dried ones *al dente* (see page 24), then drain. Heat the peanut oil in a wok or skillet and toss the cooked noodles in it until they begin to brown. Serve the vegetables on a nest of noodles.

Noodles with Snow Peas and Baby Corn

Peas and corn, both ordinary vegetables in our cooking, appear together in this dish in unusual forms. Have all the ingredients measured and ready so that the dish may be assembled very quickly and the vegetables retain their crispness.

**3 cups snow peas,* trimmed and washed
1 jar or can (15 ounces) baby corn *
1 pound linguine or fresh Chinese flat noodles *
2 tablespoons peanut oil
3 scallions, chopped
2 tablespoons soy sauce *
½ teaspoon granulated sugar
1 teaspoon sesame oil *
½ teaspoon red wine vinegar
3 tablespoons oyster sauce *
1 tablespoon cornstarch dissolved in ¼ cup water**

Blanch the snow peas by pouring boiling water over them in a colander; follow with cold water and drain well. Drain the baby corn.

Cook the noodles *al dente* (see page 24) and drain. Heat the peanut oil in a wok, add the drained noodles, and stir-fry until some are browned. Add the scallions, soy sauce, sugar, and sesame oil and continue stirring. Add the snow peas and corn.

Combine the vinegar, oyster sauce, cornstarch and water mixture, and add, stirring, to the noodles. Serve at once, with extra soy sauce if desired.

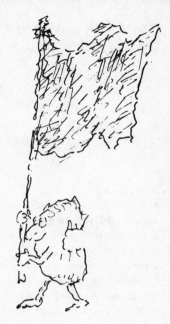

Cold Soba with Bean Curd

Soba, the light green buckwheat noodles, are commonly served cold in the summer. With cubes of bean curd, they are a favorite treat in Japan.

1 pound *soba* noodles *
2 pads bean curd,* cut into ½-inch cubes
3 scallions, chopped
2 tablespoons sesame seeds, toasted carefully in a
dry skillet
1 teaspoon sesame oil *
1 tablespoon rice wine vinegar *
1 tablespoon soy sauce *
½ teaspoon granulated sugar
½ teaspoon salt
½ teaspoon *aonoriko* (dried, pulverized seaweed)
(optional)

Cook the noodles *al dente* (see page 24), then drain in colander and cool by running cold water through them. Place in a bowl of cold water in refrigerator until almost ready to serve.

Place the cold noodles, drained, in a serving bowl and top with the bean curd cubes, scallions, and toasted sesame seeds.

Combine the remaining ingredients. Just before serving, pour the sauce over the noodles and toss very lightly.

Note: This is a dish meant to be "slurped" up: the noise of eating noodles in Japan is perfectly good manners!

Japanese Summer Somen

The *soba-ya* (noodle restaurants) of Japan serve some wonderful steamy noodles in the winter, but in the summer they produce lovely cooling noodle dishes. These, with a vegetable garnish, are served with ice cubes.

1 pound *somen* (wheat noodles) *

Sauce

6 tablespoons light soy sauce *
2 teaspoons rice wine vinegar *
2 tablespoons granulated sugar
1 teaspoon sesame oil *
1 cup defatted chicken stock

Garnishes (*to taste*)

Sansho pepper * or *togarashi* **(hot red pepper)** *
Chopped fresh coriander

Chopped scallion
Cucumber shreds
Spicy Japanese pickled vegetables *
Shredded fresh ginger *

Boil the noodles *al dente* (see page 24), then drain in colander and cool by running cold water through them. Set aside in a bowl of cold water in the refrigerator until almost ready to serve.

Heat the sauce ingredients just enough to dissolve sugar, then chill.

Just before serving, drain the noodles and divide between 6 bowls. Arrange your choice of garnishes over the noodles and pour the sauce over each. Serve with an ice cube in each bowl.

Tibetan Tomato Sauce with Noodles

Khancha, the Tibetan cook of a friend in Nepal, would serve us delicious *momos*, meat-filled dumplings, with this sauce. She also said it was good with thin egg noodles, a staple Tibetan food, and it is.

2 tablespoons mustard oil or peanut oil
1 small onion, finely chopped
1 teaspoon fenugreek seed *
4 tomatoes, peeled, seeded, and chopped (see
page 51)
Cayenne pepper to taste
3 tablespoons chopped fresh coriander or 1 teaspoon
ground coriander
Salt to taste
1 pound fine egg noodles, fresh * **or dried**

Heat the oil in a saucepan and sauté the onion until golden. Add the fenugreek seeds and sauté, stirring, for 3 minutes longer. Add the chopped tomatoes, coriander, cayenne, and salt, and simmer, partially covered, for 30 minutes. (If the sauce dries out, add a little water.) Serve over the noodles, boiled *al dente* (see page 24).

Fried Indian Noodles with Vegetable Garnishes

A halfway recipe that shows the crossed noodle paths of India and China. The vegetables are to be crisp like Chinese vegetables, yet the combination, with garnishes, is quite Indian. Still, it seems more appropriate to eat it with chopsticks!

1 pound egg noodles fresh Chinese * or dried
1 tablespoon mustard oil or vegetable oil
5 tablespoons peanut oil
½ pound green beans, ends removed and sliced in
1-inch pieces
½ cup shelled peas
½ pound cabbage, finely shredded
2 tablespoons shredded fresh ginger *
3 fresh green chilies, shredded
4 scallions, chopped
Salt and freshly ground pepper to taste
2 cups corn oil for deep frying
3 tablespoons chopped fresh coriander or 1 teaspoon
ground coriander
3 tablespoons sliced, roasted almonds
½ cup raisins, sautéed briefly in 2 tablespoons butter

Boil the egg noodles *al dente* (see page 24), then toss with the mustard or vegetable oil and let cool.

Heat the peanut oil in a skillet. Add the beans, peas, cabbage, ginger, and chilies, one at a time, frying over high heat for 2 or 3 minutes, and stirring well each time a vegetable is added. Add the scallions, toss, and remove from the heat. Add salt and pepper to taste.

In a large skillet or wok, heat the corn oil to 350 degrees on a deep-frying thermometer and fry the noodles in handfuls, removing to paper towels when crisp and golden. Place the noodles on a serving platter and top with the mixed vegetables. Garnish with the coriander, almonds, and raisins and serve.

Korean Noodles with Pine Nuts

Korean noodle dishes have a subtle sweetness. This one is excellent served with broiled foods, like the famous *bul kogi*—grilled beef strips with sesame seeds and garlic.

3 cups very thin vermicelli, broken into bits
2 tablespoons peanut oil
¾ cup blanched, slivered almonds
½ cup pignoli (pine nuts)
2 tablespoons honey
2 tablespoons soy sauce *

Boil the vermicelli *al dente* (see page 24) and drain well.

Heat the oil in a heavy skillet and brown the nuts and pignoli in it, stirring. Add to the noodles, along with the honey and soy sauce, tossing with forks. Serve immediately.

Baingan Tamatar (Eggplant and Tomato Curry with Noodles)

Although a "curry," this dish has no "curry" spices. It is a relatively light vegetable mixture with browned noodles. It should, however, be "hot" with cayenne and chilies.

1 pound very thin egg noodles
1 medium eggplant (about 1 pound)
Salt
2 tablespoons butter or mustard oil
2 medium onions, thinly sliced
1 green pepper, seeded and diced
½ teaspoon freshly ground black pepper
½ teaspoon cayenne pepper
6 ripe tomatoes, peeled, seeded, and sliced (see page 51)
2 fresh green chilies, shredded (optional)
2 tablespoons vegetable oil
2 tablespoons chopped fresh coriander or parsley

Boil the noodles *al dente* (see page 24), then drain and let cool.

Peel the eggplant, then cut into small chunks. Sprinkle with 1 tablespoon salt and let stand in a colander, over a bowl or sink, for 30 minutes. Dry on paper towels.

Heat the butter or oil in a large skillet and stir-fry the onion and green pepper until the onion is golden. Add the black pepper and cayenne and stir, then add the eggplant. Cover and cook over slow heat until almost tender.

Add the tomatoes, green chilies, and salt to taste, then cover and cook, stirring frequently, until the tomatoes and eggplant are done.

Heat the vegetable oil in a wok. Add the cooled noodles and fry, stirring, over high heat until some are browned.

Place the noodles in a serving bowl and toss with the eggplant mixture. Garnish with the fresh coriander or parsley and serve.

Burmese Tomato Curry with Noodles

Burmese food is, unfortunately, little known in this country. It combines aspects of both Indian and Chinese cooking, but emphasizes special tastes, like deep-fried garlic and fish sauce, which distinguish it from these more familiar cuisines. The recipe below presents a delightful version of tomato sauce.

3 pounds tomatoes, peeled, seeded, and chopped (see page 51)
3 tablespoons peanut or mustard oil
4 medium onions, very thinly sliced
3 cloves garlic, minced
Salt to taste
1 teaspoon ground turmeric
1 teaspoon ground coriander
½ teaspoon crushed dried red chilies *
1 tablespoon fish sauce *
12 ounces thin egg noodles

Heat the oil in a heavy saucepan. Add the sliced onion and garlic and sauté until golden; then add the tomatoes, salt, turmeric, coriander, crushed dried red chilies, and fish sauce and cook over very low heat for 20 to 30 minutes.

Boil the noodles *al dente* (see page 24), then drain well, toss with the tomato mixture, and serve.

Fideos con Salsa de nuez

An Argentine friend gave this recipe to me. It reminds me of a walnut *pesto,* but with refinements: the *crème fraîche* at the beginning, and the essential homemade egg noodles. Quite a filling dish.

2 pounds noodles, made from Fresh Egg Pasta (see pages 19–21)
¼ cup each sour cream and heavy cream, mixed
Salt and freshly ground black pepper
3 tablespoons butter
2 cloves garlic, finely minced
1 cup finely chopped walnuts
1 cup freshly grated Parmesan cheese
½ cup chicken broth

Boil the noodles *al dente* (see page 24), then drain well and toss with the mixed creams (an approximation of *crème fraîche,* which you should use instead if you have it), salt and pepper to taste, and 2 tablespoons of the butter. Cover and keep warm.

Heat the remaining tablespoon butter in a small saucepan. Sauté the garlic for 3 minutes; be careful not to let it brown. Remove from the heat, then stir in the walnuts, Parmesan, and chicken broth, and toss with the noodles. Serve immediately.

Mushroom Noodle Casserole

Mushrooms, baked with noodles, are quite delicious. Like other casserole noodle dishes, this one can be assembled ahead of time and baked later. It can even be frozen before baking.

4 tablespoons (½ stick) butter
2 cups sliced fresh mushrooms
2 teaspoons lemon juice
1 clove garlic, minced
¼ cup freshly grated Parmesan cheese
Salt and freshly ground pepper to taste
8 ounces rotini or other macaroni
2 eggs, lightly beaten
1 cup milk
1 tablespoon all-purpose flour
¼ cup bread crumbs

Preheat the oven to 375 degrees.

Melt 2 tablespoons of the butter in a skillet. Add the mushrooms and cook, stirring, for 5 minutes, then add the lemon juice, garlic, Parmesan, and salt and pepper to taste. Set aside.

Boil the noodles *al dente* (see page 24). Drain well.

In a bowl combine the eggs, milk, flour, and salt and pepper to taste. Beat well, then combine with the mushrooms and fold into the noodles. Pour into a buttered casserole. Sprinkle with the bread crumbs and dot with the remaining 2 tablespoons butter. Bake in the preheated oven for 30 minutes, or until bubbly and browned.

Ratatouille with Noodles

Ratatouille is a wonderful summer staple. Good cold or hot, it is splendid on pasta and improves upon a day or two's rest in the refrigerator. With eggplant, zucchini, and tomatoes as a base, you can experiment by adding other vegetables in season. Ratatouille reminds me of a one-shot *Rumtopf,* that endless alcoholic pot to which one adds fruits as they ripen all summer to make a pungent compote by fall.

1 medium eggplant, peeled and cut into small cubes
3 medium zucchini, scrubbed and sliced
Salt
6 tablespoons olive oil
3 onions, coarsely chopped
2 green peppers, seeded and diced
3 cloves garlic, finely minced
1 bay leaf
2 pounds ripe tomatoes, peeled, seeded, and
chopped (see page 51)
½ cup chopped fresh parsley
½ teaspoon dried thyme
1 tablespoon chopped fresh basil or 1 teaspoon
dried
1 pound egg noodles

Place the eggplant and zucchini in a large colander over
the sink or a kettle. Salt well and toss, then leave to drain
for 1 hour.

In a large skillet or saucepan, heat the oil. Sauté the
onion and green pepper until the onion is golden, then
add the garlic, bay leaf, and tomatoes and simmer for 10
minutes. Add the eggplant and zucchini, after rinsing with
cold water and patting dry. Simmer for 10 minutes, then
add the parsley, thyme, and basil and simmer for 20
minutes more.

Boil the noodles *al dente* (see page 24), then drain.
Toss with the *ratatouille* mixture and serve.

Black Beans and Macaroni

This much garlic may seem like a lot, but in the cooking it
loses its pungency and adds a very savory nuttiness to the
rich bean and macaroni combination. I'm not sure of

this recipe's ethnic origins, but it is probably from the southern United States or from Central America.

2 cups dried black beans, soaked overnight and drained
1 head garlic, separated into cloves, then peeled and minced
½ pound salt pork, finely diced
1 pound elbow macaroni or small shells
1 tablespoon ground cumin
1 tablespoon salt
Freshly ground pepper to taste

Cook the beans slowly, in water to cover plus 2 cloves of the head of garlic, until tender. Drain, saving the liquid.

Preheat the oven to 325 degrees.

In a heavy skillet, sauté the salt pork until crisp and golden. Remove with a slotted spoon onto paper towels. Add the remaining garlic to the fat in the skillet and sauté over very low heat, until soft.

Boil the noodles *al dente* (see page 24), then drain and toss with the beans, together with the salt pork and garlic, cumin, salt, and pepper. Pour into a casserole, add a little of the liquid from the beans, then bake in the oven, covered, for about 1 hour.

Green Noodle Soufflé

If you can find green vermicelli, use it. Otherwise the green is from the spinach, parsley, and scallions in the recipe, which makes a substantial vegetable dish to plan a meal around.

8 ounces vermicelli
2 packages (10 ounces each) frozen spinach,

defrosted, drained, and finely chopped
½ cup chopped fresh parsley
¼ cup finely chopped scallions
1 cup freshly grated Parmesan cheese
¼ cup melted butter
Salt and freshly ground black pepper to taste
4 eggs, separated

Preheat the oven to 350 degrees.

Break the vermicelli into small pieces and boil *al dente* (see page 24). Drain well.

Combine the spinach, parsley, scallions, drained vermicelli, Parmesan, butter, salt, pepper and egg yolks.

Beat the egg whites until stiff, then, very gently, fold them into the spinach mixture. Pour into a greased casserole and bake for 40 minutes, or until set and browned.

Carol and Lynn Karlson's Vegetable Spaghetti

This dish is an improvisation of two graduate students who found that their budget called for many meatless meals. I used regular spaghetti when I made it, but I'm sure it would also be delicious with a short broad noodle, or with shells.

1 pound spaghetti
1 bunch broccoli, washed and separated into
small florets
½ pound fresh mushrooms
3 cloves of minced garlic
2 tablespoons butter
2 tablespoons olive oil
Salt and freshly ground pepper to taste
1 cup freshly grated Gruyère cheese

In two pots of boiling salted water, cook the spaghetti and broccoli simultaneously for 8 minutes, or until both are *al dente*.

Meanwhile, sauté the mushrooms and garlic in the butter and oil.

Drain the spaghetti and broccoli in separate colanders, then toss together in a serving bowl, along with the mushrooms and their sautéing mixture, salt, pepper, and Gruyère. Serve immediately.

Spaghetti Crown with Mushroom Sauce

A luncheon dish, but a rather elegant one; it rather reminds me of molded buffet dishes from the thirties. Though I don't know its provenance, I would guess that it is Scandinavian in origin.

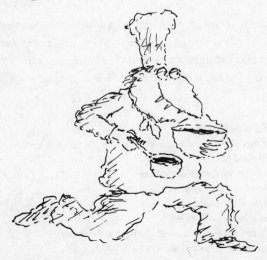

8 ounces vermicelli
1 teaspoon butter
1 teaspoon all-purpose flour
½ cup milk
1 tablespoon heavy cream
1 egg, beaten
⅓ cup freshly grated Parmesan cheese
Salt, freshly ground pepper, and nutmeg to taste
Mushroom Sauce (see below)

Preheat the oven to 350 degrees.

Boil the noodles *al dente* (see page 24), then drain well.

Make a white sauce by melting the butter in a small saucepan, stirring in the flour, and adding milk; simmer, stirring until thickened. Combine the heavy cream and beaten egg and add a little sauce to it. Then, beating constantly, add the cream mixture to the hot sauce and heat carefully for a minute or two.

Fold the sauce into the drained noodles and pour into

a greased ring mold. Place the mold in a roasting pan and fill the pan with boiling water to a point halfway up the side of the mold. Bake for 30 minutes, or until set.

Meanwhile, make the mushroom sauce. When the noodle ring is ready, unmold onto a serving platter. Pour the mushroom sauce into the center of the ring and serve.

Mushroom Sauce

½ pound fresh mushrooms, sliced
1 tablespoon minced shallots
½ cup dry white wine, more if necessary
4 tablespoons (½ stick) softened butter
2 tablespoons all-purpose flour
1 tablespoon lemon juice
¼ cup heavy cream
1 egg yolk, beaten
Salt and freshly ground pepper to taste

Cook the mushrooms, shallots, and wine together for 10 minutes, then drain, reserving the wine.

Cream together the butter and flour. Add to the wine in a small saucepan and cook until thickened, adding more wine if the mixture is too thick. Add the lemon juice, cream, egg yolk, and mushrooms and cook, stirring, until thickened. Add salt and pepper to taste.

FISH AND SHELLFISH

Fish and Shellfish

Shrimp, Ricotta, and Vermicelli

Pink and white, shrimp and ricotta go well with very thin noodles. This is a very quick dish, which can be assembled in 10 minutes, should you have peeled shrimps around.

½ pound raw shrimps, peeled and deveined
2 tablespoons olive oil
1 teaspoon chopped fresh basil or ½ teaspoon dried
1 pound vermicelli
3 tablespoons melted butter
8 ounces ricotta cheese
Salt and freshly ground black pepper to taste
2 tablespoons chopped fresh parsley
½ cup freshly grated Parmesan cheese

In a small skillet, sauté the shrimps in the oil and toss with the basil. Set aside.

Boil the vermicelli *al dente* (see page 24), then drain well. Place in a warm bowl with 2 tablespoons of the melted butter.

Place the ricotta in a pan and stir, with 1 tablespoon of the butter, over low heat until smooth and warm, then pour over the hot vermicelli. Top with the shrimps, salt, pepper, parsley, and grated cheese and toss. Serve immediately.

Mussels Leopardo

Mussels have been considered in the past a "poor" scavenger sort of dish, scarcely deserving of cookbook mention. They are a bit more trouble to clean than clams, for the "beard" should be scraped off, but to me they are more flavorful and interesting than clams. Italian cooks have recognized this for a long time.

3 pounds mussels, well cleaned and debearded
½ cup olive oil
3 cloves garlic, chopped
1 large can (35 ounce size) tomatoes in purée,
chopped well
½ teaspoon salt
1 bay leaf
½ teaspoon dried thyme
2 tablespoons finely chopped fresh parsley
Crushed dried red chilies * to taste
Freshly ground pepper to taste
½ cup dry white wine or water
1 pound vermicelli

Place the oil in a large pot. Add the garlic and sauté until browned, then add the tomatoes, salt, bay leaf, thyme, parsley, red chilies, black pepper, and simmer for 5 minutes. Add the ½ cup wine or water, and bring to a boil. Add the mussels and cover the pot.

When all the mussels are open, set aside briefly, covered, while you boil the vermicelli *al dente* (see page 24). Drain the pasta, place in large soup bowls, and top with the mussel mixture. Serve with garlic toast rounds.

Rigatoni with Squid

A peppery squid sauce is a favorite in Italy. I like it best with large, firm noodles like rigatoni.

Squid should be cleaned under running water. Pull out the head and tentacles and the clear cartilage (which looks like a piece of plastic), then carefully pull off the purplish translucent skin.

¼ cup olive oil
1 pound fresh squid, cleaned, skinned, and cut into wide pieces
2 cloves garlic, minced
1 green pepper, seeded and roughly chopped
3 fresh green chilies, seeded and finely chopped
Salt and red pepper flakes to taste
1 large can (35 ounce size) tomatoes, roughly chopped
1 can (6 ounces) tomato paste
1 pound rigatoni

Heat the oil in a heavy skillet over medium heat. Sauté the squid until curled, then add the garlic and lower the heat a little. Add the green pepper, chilies, red pepper flakes, tomatoes, and tomato paste and simmer for 15 minutes. If too thick, add water; if not thick enough, let simmer until thickened.

Cook the rigatoni *al dente,* then drain well, place in a serving bowl, and top with the sauce. Serve immediately.

Spaghetti with Sardines

An interesting combination of tastes—the bland, crunchy pignoli with the two fishy tastes, as well as garlic, pasta, and raisins. This dish is traditionally served at Epiphany in Italy.

3 tablespoons olive oil
½ cup pignoli (pine nuts)
3 small tins sardines, chopped
2 cloves garlic, minced
2 small tins (2 ounces each) anchovies, mashed
¼ cup raisins (optional)
2 tablespoons chopped fresh parsley
1 pound spaghetti

Heat the olive oil in a heavy skillet and lightly brown the pignoli in it. Add the sardines, garlic, and anchovies and sauté for 4 minutes, stirring well. Add the raisins, if used, and the parsley.

Boil the spaghetti *al dente* (see page 24), then drain and toss with the sardine mixture. Serve immediately.

Fettucine with Seafood Sauce

A wonderful one-dish meal that needs only a very plain salad and a crusty bread as an accompaniment. Good for summer eating when clams and mussels can be dug fresh.

½ cup olive oil
1 small onion, minced
2 cloves garlic, minced

2 tablespoons minced fresh parsley
1 teaspoon salt
Freshly ground black pepper to taste
1 teaspoon finely chopped fresh thyme or ½
teaspoon dried
2 cups heavy cream
½ cup dry white wine
½ pound medium raw shrimps, peeled and deveined
½ pound bay scallops (optional)
8 to 10 littleneck clams, scrubbed
2 pounds mussels, well scrubbed and debearded
1 pound fettucine, freshly made (see pages
19–21) if possible

Heat the oil in heavy skillet. Add the onion and garlic and sauté until soft; do not let burn. Add the parsley, salt, pepper, thyme, cream, and wine and bring to a boil. Let boil for 5 to 8 minutes over high heat, then reduce the heat to medium and add the shrimps, scallops, clams, and mussels. Cook, covered, until the shells open.

Meanwhile, boil the fettucine *al dente* (see page 24), then drain and place in a large serving dish. Pour the sauce over, arranging the clams and mussels over the top. Serve immediately.

Spaghetti al Tonno

Italian pasta recipes often use tuna, and in far more interesting ways than our "tuna casseroles." This recipe has a nice piquant flavor, due to its capers and anchovies. You could serve it with lemon wedges.

1/4 cup olive oil
2 cloves garlic, finely minced
2 pounds tomatoes, peeled, seeded, and chopped
(see page 51)
1 tablespoon finely chopped fresh basil or 1
teaspoon dried
1 can (7 ounces) tuna, drained and flaked
2 tablespoons capers
1 teaspoon minced anchovy or anchovy paste
Salt and freshly ground pepper to taste
1 pound spaghetti

In a heavy saucepan, heat the olive oil and sauté the garlic until lightly browned. Add the tomatoes and basil and simmer for 30 minutes, adding water if necessary. Add the tuna, capers, anchovies, and salt and pepper to taste.

Boil the spaghetti *al dente* (see page 24), then drain, place in a serving bowl, and pour the sauce over. Serve immediately.

Vermicelli with Clam and Broccoli Sauce

Just as scallops and broccoli are complementary, so are clams and broccoli in a light garlicky sauce. Again, the warning to *undercook* the broccoli is important.

1 bunch fresh broccoli, washed and separated into
florets
1/2 cup olive oil
2 cloves garlic, peeled and sliced
2 cans (7 1/2 ounces each) minced clams, juice
reserved

½ teaspoon salt
Freshly ground black pepper to taste
½ teaspoon dried oregano
1 pound vermicelli
2 tablespoons chopped fresh coriander or parsley
½ cup freshly grated Romano cheese

Boil the broccoli for 4 or 5 minutes in a large kettle of water, then taste; when you can just bite through the stem, the broccoli is done. Drain well and run cold water through it.

In a heavy skillet, heat the olive oil and sauté the garlic for 2 minutes, stirring. Add the reserved clam juice, salt, pepper, and oregano. Add the clams and broccoli and cook, stirring, for a few minutes, until heated through.

Boil the vermicelli *al dente* (see page 24) and drain well. Stir the parsley or coriander into the sauce and toss with the vermicelli. Serve, sprinkled with the freshly grated Romano.

Simple White Clam Sauce

Clam sauce using canned clams is very quick and a very good "larder" meal, since you can keep the main ingredients on hand indefinitely. You could use cans of baby whole clams instead, or one each of minced and whole, for a more interesting texture.

2 tablespoons olive oil
4 cloves garlic, finely minced
2 cans minced (7½ ounce size) clams, juice of one can reserved
½ cup dry white wine

½ teaspoon dried thyme
6 tablespoons minced fresh parsley
12 ounces linguine
2 tablespoons butter
Salt and freshly ground pepper to taste

Heat the oil in skillet and sauté the garlic briefly, until golden. Add the clams, the reserved juice, and wine and cook rapidly, to reduce the liquid, for 3 minutes. Lower the heat, add the thyme, parsley, salt, and pepper and set aside.

Boil the linguine *al dente* (see page 24) and toss first with the butter, then with the clam sauce. Serve at once.

Clams with Tomato Sauce and Spaghetti

Red clam sauce for pasta is excellent, and much heartier than the white variety. My own opinion is that the heavy sauce rather overwhelms the clams, but if you use the *whole* clams they hold their own.

2 medium onions, minced
2 tablespoons olive oil
1 can (35 ounces) tomatoes
1 can (6 ounces) tomato paste
2 cloves garlic, pressed
1 tablespoon chopped fresh basil or 1 teaspoon dried
2 teaspoons granulated sugar
Salt and freshly ground black pepper to taste
1 can (12 ounces) whole baby clams, juice reserved

3 ounces fresh mushrooms, sliced
1 pound spaghetti
Freshly grated Parmesan cheese to taste

Sauté the onion in the oil until soft. Add the tomatoes and tomato paste, crushing the tomatoes with a spoon; then add the garlic, basil, sugar, salt, and pepper and let simmer briefly. Add the clams, with the reserved liquid, and the mushrooms. Boil the sauce down if too thin, then let simmer for at least 30 minutes.

Meanwhile, boil the spaghetti *al dente* (see page 24) and drain. Pour the sauce on individual servings of spaghetti and top with grated Parmesan.

Vermicelli with Tomato Sauce and Anchovies

A very simple anchovy sauce—another "larder" dish, the ingredients of which you can have on hand for improvised suppers.

3 cloves garlic, chopped
3 tablespoons olive oil
2 tablespoons chopped chives
2 cans (2 ounces each) anchovy fillets, chopped
1 can (35 ounces) tomatoes
1 can (6 ounces) tomato paste
1 pound vermicelli
Salt and freshly ground pepper to taste

In a skillet, sauté the garlic in the oil until it turns golden. Add the chives and the chopped anchovies and sauté briefly, stirring, then add the tomatoes and the tomato

paste, crushing the tomatoes with a wooden spoon. Add salt and pepper to taste and let the sauce simmer for at least 30 minutes.

Meanwhile, cook the vermicelli *al dente* (see page 24), then drain and toss with the tomato sauce. Serve immediately.

Spinach-Anchovy Cannelloni

Forgetting to bone the large anchovies I bought in an Italian market, I "crunched" through my first trial of this dish. *Without* the bones, this is an excellent variation of the usual cheesy filling. These *cannelloni,* made with lasagne noodles, are not as delicate as the freshly made variety, but are very good and seem to suit the robust filling.

2 tablespoons olive oil
2 medium onions, finely chopped
3 cloves garlic, finely chopped

**5 large anchovies, boned, or 1 can (2 ounces)
small anchovies, both chopped fine
2 tablespoons finely chopped peperoni
1 package (10 ounces) fresh spinach, washed,
drained, and picked over
Salt and freshly ground black pepper to taste
¼ cup freshly grated Parmesan cheese
8 ounces lasagne noodles
8 ounces mozzarella, roughly grated**

Heat the oil in a large, heavy skillet. Add the onion and garlic and sauté until golden, then add the anchovies and peperoni and sauté for 1 minute. Place the spinach on top, cover, and cook, checking after 3 minutes to stir the spinach down. Cover again and cook until the spinach is wilted, then remove from the heat and add salt, pepper, and the Parmesan, and set aside.

Preheat the oven to 375 degrees.

In a large kettle, boil the noodles until just tender, then drain. Separate the noodles and toss with oil to keep from sticking; be careful not to tear them. Then, using ½ noodle at a time, place 2 tablespoons of the filling mixture on the noodle and roll it up. Place the stuffed rolls on a buttered baking dish in one layer. Top with the grated mozzarella, then bake in the preheated oven until heated through, and until the cheese is bubbly on top.

Vermicelli with Clam Sauce
à la Crème

This is an adaptation of a clam sauce culled from a woman's magazine some time ago. The addition of cream to the simple clam sauce makes this very elegant.

2 pounds steamer clams
1 pound vermicelli
4 tablespoons (½ stick) butter
1 cup medium cream
¼ cup freshly grated Parmesan cheese
Salt and freshly ground black pepper to taste
2 tablespoons chopped fresh parsley

Clean the steamer clams, then steam them open in ½ inch
of water in large saucepan, covered. Remove from the pan,
but retain the liquid. Remove the clams from their shells
and pull off the sandy "neck" skins. Chop the clams
roughly and set aside.

Boil the vermicelli *al dente* (see page 24) and drain
well. In a heavy saucepan, heat the butter. Add the vermicelli and toss with the cream and Parmesan until hot. Add
the clams, reserved clam liquid, salt, and pepper, tossing.
Serve immediately, with more Parmesan if desired and
the parsley as a garnish.

Escargots with Pasta

6 first-course servings

Snails in snail butter are here given a noodle treatment
and the garlicky parsley butter is perfect for both. This is
especially good for a first course, for which the following
recipe is designed (with amounts adjusted for smaller portions for six people).

12 ounces thin spaghetti
¾ cup (1½ sticks) butter
¼ cup minced scallions
5 cloves garlic, mashed
Salt and freshly ground black pepper to taste

2 small cans escargots, drained and roughly
chopped
6 tablespoons minced fresh parsley

Boil the thin spaghetti *al dente* (see page 24).

Meanwhile, heat the butter in small saucepan. When
melted, add the scallions, garlic, and salt and pepper and
sauté over low heat for 3 minutes, stirring; do not allow
the garlic to brown. Add the drained and chopped snails
and toss, heating gently. Add the parsley.

Drain the thin spaghetti and place in a serving bowl.
Pour the snail mixture over and toss, then serve at once,
with freshly grated Parmesan cheese on the side.

Plaki

Greek fish dishes are often very hearty, and it is best to
use a fish that can stand up to the flavors of garlic, tomatoes,
and salty olives. The coarser and firmer white fish are
good; I use cod often.

¼ cup olive oil
4 medium onions, chopped
2 cloves garlic, finely minced
3 stalks celery, chopped
5 tomatoes, peeled, seeded, and sliced (see page 51)
Salt and freshly ground black pepper to taste
12 ounces elbow macaroni
2 pounds firm white fish fillets (haddock, halibut,
pollack, or cod)
¼ cup lemon juice
8 black Greek olives, pitted and chopped
¼ cup minced fresh parsley

Preheat the oven to 350 degrees.

Heat the oil in a skillet and sauté the onion until golden. Add the garlic, celery, tomatoes, and salt and pepper and sauté over low heat for 5 minutes.

Meanwhile, boil the macaroni *al dente* (see page 24). Drain, then place in a buttered casserole and put the sautéed vegetables on top. Place the fish on the vegetables, sprinkle with salt and pepper and lemon juice, and arrange the olives on top.

Bake, covered, for 30 minutes, or until the fish flakes easily with a fork. Garnish with the parsley and serve.

Scandinavian Fish Pudding

"Fish pudding" has a rather flat sound to it, but this creamy mixture is quite hearty and delicious. You might also want to add a tablespoon of capers.

2 cups cooked macaroni
2 tablespoons melted butter
1 teaspoon salt
Freshly ground black pepper
1 pound firm white fish (haddock, halibut,
pollack, or cod), cooked and separated into chunks
½ cup cream
½ cup fish or clam broth
2 eggs, separated
1 cup freshly grated Gruyère cheese
1 tablespoon chopped fresh dill
½ cup bread crumbs

Preheat the oven to 350 degrees.

Toss the macaroni with the salt, pepper, fish, butter, cream, broth, egg yolks, cheese, and dill. Beat the egg whites until stiff and pile on top of the macaroni mixture, then top with the bread crumbs and bake for 40 minutes.

Chinese Clam Sauce for Linguine or Fresh Chinese Noodles

Black beans and clams make a wonderful sauce. It is also excellent with shrimp, and is similar to the snail (periwinkle) sauce in this book (see page 141).

1 pound linguine or fresh Chinese noodles *
3 tablespoons salted, fermented black beans *
1 tablespoon red wine vinegar
1 teaspoon granulated sugar
2 tablespoons soy sauce *
2 tablespoons oyster sauce *
½ cup chicken broth, clam broth, or water
3 fresh hot chilies, seeded and finely chopped
Rind of ½ lemon, julienned in very thin strips
4 cloves garlic, finely minced
2 tablespoons chopped fresh ginger *
3 tablespoons peanut oil
¼ pound ground pork
3 pounds steamer clams, cleaned
1 tablespoon cornstarch dissolved in ¼ cup water

Boil the noodles *al dente* (see page 24), then drain well
and keep warm.

Combine the black beans, vinegar, sugar, soy sauce,
and oyster sauce. Add ½ cup chicken broth, clam broth or
water and set aside.

Combine the chilies, lemon rind, garlic, and ginger and
set aside.

Heat the oil in a wok. Add the pork and stir-fry until
browned and separated, then add the chili mixture and
stir-fry for 2 minutes. Add the black bean mixture and
stir-fry for 2 minutes more. Add the clams, cover the wok,
and cook until the clams open.

Place the clams in a large bowl, leaving the sauce in
the wok. Add the cornstarch mixture, then bring the sauce
to a boil, stirring. When thick, pour over the clams and
serve, along with the noodles.

Laksa

Laksa is a Malaysian dish that uses Chinese fishballs and a Malaysian version of curry powder, and that is all held together by the omnipresent *santan,* or pressed coconut milk. You can make quite a bit of *santan* and freeze it for future use. (The amount of curry powder sounds like a lot; but somehow the Malaysian variety is not very hot; the heat is added by the chili powder, which you should adjust to taste.) Judith Strauch brought this recipe back from Malaysia.

2 pounds *meifun* or thin noodles
3 cups bean sprouts, washed and drained
2 tablespoons peanut oil
1 teaspoon salt
6 tablespoons Malaysian curry powder, or
3 tablespoons Madras curry powder
3 teaspoons chili powder, or to taste
3 ½ cups water
6 tablespoons tamarind * soaked in ½ cup warm water
4 chicken bouillon cubes
2 cups Santan (see below)
2 cans Chinese fishballs *
1 cup finely ground peanuts
2 cucumbers, peeled, cut in half lengthwise and seeded, then cut in thin strips
4 fresh chilies, seeded and cut into very thin shreds
3 pads bean curd,* pressed between two plates to remove excess liquid and cubed
3 eggs, hard boiled
2 limes, cut in wedges
1 purple onion, in thin rings

Boil noodles *al dente* (see page 24). Drain well, then place in a serving bowl or in individual bowls.

In large kettle of boiling water, parboil the bean sprouts for 1 minute, then drain well in a colander. Run cold water through them and set aside.

Heat the oil in a wok or heavy skillet. Add the salt, curry powder, chili powder, and ½ cup of the water. Stir into a paste and fry for 2 minutes, stirring.

Drain the tamarind over a small bowl, squeezing to extract the liquid. Add the tamarind water to the paste and boil until reduced to a paste again.

Place the paste in large kettle. Add the 3 cups water, the chicken bouillon cubes, the coconut liquid, and the fishballs, drained. Heat through, just to the boiling point, then add the ground peanuts.

Pour the "soup" over the noodles, dividing the fishballs evenly, and serve. Accompany with a plate of the garnishes, or garnish each bowl separately with the following: the cucumber strips, chili shreds, hard-boiled eggs (cut in quarters), lime wedges, onion rings, and bean curd cubes (deep-fried in peanut oil and golden if desired).

Santan

Soak 1 cup grated fresh coconut or unsweetened coconut shreds in 3 cups warm water for 15 minutes, then squeeze through a cloth into a bowl until you have 2 cups liquid.

Pathai

This is a Thai noodle dish, one of a great tradition. Jane Siegel, who lived in Bangkok for several years, provided this recipe. The noodles to be used are cellophane or rice noodles, which come in swirls or twists in Thailand, but are also available in Chinese markets in small skeins.

Peanut oil as needed
1 cup raw peanuts, skinned
3 heads garlic, separated into cloves, then peeled and sliced
¼ pound pork tenderloin, shredded
2 cups medium raw shrimps, peeled and deveined
2 pads bean curd *
1 pound cellophane noodles,* soaked in warm water and drained
¼ cup dried shrimp,* soaked in warm water
2 tablespoons fish sauce *
1 tablespoon vinegar
1 teaspoon granulated sugar
2 eggs, beaten lightly
Lime wedges for garnish

Brush a heavy skillet with peanut oil and place the skinned peanuts in it over medium heat, shaking the pan occasionally to brown the peanuts evenly. Set the peanuts aside.

Add 2 or 3 tablespoons of oil to the pan and fry the garlic cloves until brown and crisp—but *do not let them burn*. Remove with a slotted spoon and drain on paper towels. Add the pork strips to the pan and cook, stirring, until brown, then add the shrimps and stir until curled and cooked.

Add the bean curd, cut into cubes, and the noodles, then add ½ cup water or so and cover to steam the noodles for about 1 minute. Add the dried shrimp, drained, and the fish sauce, vinegar, and sugar. Add the garlic bits.

In a small skillet, scramble the eggs, then cut them into bits and add to the pan. Arrange all the ingredients on a platter and garnish with the peanuts. Serve with lime wedges.

Unagi Donburi

Unagi donburi, or broiled eel on a bowl of rice—a very common and delicious Japanese dish—loses nothing in its translation into a noodle dish. The sauce, slurped up with *soba* noodles, is lovely when the eel or fish juices have dripped into it.

¾ pound mackerel or eel, cleaned, boned, and filleted
½ cup plus 2 tablespoons soy sauce *
2 tablespoons plus 1 teaspoon sesame oil *
2½ teaspoons granulated sugar
1 teaspoon *aonoriko* (dried, pulverized seaweed) *
(optional)
1 pound thin *soba* noodles *
2 tablespoons rice wine vinegar *
2 scallions, finely chopped

Marinate mackerel or eel with the 2 tablespoons soy sauce, 1 teaspoon of the sesame oil, and ½ teaspoon of the sugar for 30 minutes, then sprinkle with aonoriko (optional) and broil for 10 minutes, or until done.

Meanwhile, boil the *soba* noodles *al dente* (see page 00) and drain them; combine the ½ cup soy sauce, 2 tablespoons sesame oil, 2 teaspoons sugar, and vinegar and set aside.

Divide noodles among individual serving bowls. Cut the fish into bowl-sized segments and place on top. Garnish with the scallions.

Each diner pours sauce over his fish and noodles.

Chinese Periwinkles with Linguine

This is my favorite of all snail recipes, Chinese or other-wise. We take expeditions every summer to get them from a restaurant that has made its reputation (for us, at least) on this dish alone. The slight fuss in eating them, picking them out of the shell and discarding the hard, flat disc off the end before eating, is well worth it, and gives the meal a pleasant leisurely quality.

1 tablespoon granulated sugar
1 teaspoon salt
1 tablespoon cornstarch
2 tablespoons salted, fermented black beans,*
washed and mashed with a fork
2 tablespoons soy sauce *
2 tablespoons hoisin sauce *
½ teaspoon crushed dried red peppers,*
or to taste
2 to 3 pounds periwinkles
3 tablespoons peanut oil
2 teaspoons sesame oil *
1½ tablespoons fresh finely chopped ginger *
2 cloves garlic, minced
5 scallions, finely chopped
3 fresh green chilies, shredded
¼ cup dry sherry
1 cup chicken broth
1 pound linguine or fresh Chinese flat noodles *

Combine the sugar, salt, cornstarch, mashed black beans, soy sauce, hoisin sauce, and dried red peppers. Set aside.

Soak the periwinkle in cold water for 1 hour, scrub-bing them by rubbing them together under water, and changing the water often. Smell them one by one for freshness.

Heat a wok. Add the peanut and sesame oils, then the ginger, garlic, scallions, and fresh chilies. Add the sherry and simmer for 1 minute, then add the snails, and stir-fry for 2 minutes. Add the reserved seasoning mixture and the broth and bring to a simmer, stirring. Let simmer for 5 minutes.

Boil the noodles *al dente* (see page 24), then drain well and place in a large bowl. Serve the snails and sauce over the noodles.

Note: Provide long hat pins for getting the snails out of their shells.

Soba Noodles with Tempura

In Japan, *tempura soba* is quite popular as a lunch or evening snack, and the most popular tempura is shrimp. Serve tempura as quickly as possible after frying it. It should be eaten off the top of the noodles and not dunked, for it becomes soggy quickly.

1 egg yolk
1 cup ice water
1 cup plus 1 tablespoon all-purpose flour
1 cup chicken broth
1 tablespoon finely chopped fresh ginger *
2 tablespoons dry sherry
2 tablespoons soy sauce *
Vegetable oil for deep frying
6 large fresh mushrooms
1 green pepper, seeded and cut into strips
½ pound medium raw shrimps, peeled and deveined
1 pound *soba* noodles * boiled *al dente* (see page 24) and drained

¼ cup grated fresh *daikon* (long white
horseradish) *
1 tablespoon granulated sugar

Prepare a batter by placing the egg yolk in a bowl. Beat
it well, adding the ice water while beating, then the flour
all at once. Beat only briefly after the flour is added, for
the batter should be lumpy. Set aside.

Heat together, in a small saucepan, the chicken broth,
sugar, sherry, and soy sauce. Heat just until the sugar dis-
solves, then set aside.

Heat the oil in a deep frying pot or wok. Let one drop
of tempura batter drip in; if it rises quickly and browns
lightly in less than a minute, the oil is hot enough. Dip
the vegetables and shrimp in the batter and fry, a few at a
time, until golden. Drain on paper towels.

While the fried foods are draining, divide the noodles
between 6 individual bowls. Add the grated *daikon* and
ginger and pour the hot sauce over each. Place an assortment of tempura on each bowl and serve.

Shrimp Patia with Vermicelli

Shrimp Patia is an Indian dish I first had in London, and I
have been searching for that taste ever since. I have here
put together several versions of it in an approximation of
my first experience.

½ teaspoon salt
1 teaspoon ground cumin
½ teaspoon crushed hot red pepper

3 tablespoons corn oil
1 tablespoon peanut oil
2 cups sliced onion
1 green pepper, finely chopped
1 teaspoon finely chopped fresh ginger *
3 cloves garlic, finely chopped
4 fresh green chilies, finely chopped
1 pound raw shrimp, peeled and deveined,
combined with ½ teaspoon ground turmeric
1 can (12 ounces) Italian tomatoes in puree,
roughly chopped
¼ cup water
1 pound vermicelli
Chopped fresh coriander for garnish

Heat a heavy skillet. Stir the salt, cumin, and crushed hot red pepper in it over high heat for one minute, then lower the heat, add the two oils and the onion and green pepper and stir for 5 minutes, until the onion is wilted.

Add the ginger, garlic, and chilies and stir for another minute, then add the shrimp and stir until they turn pink and curl up. Add the tomatoes and the ¼ cup water and stir. Let simmer until the mixture is fairly thick.

Boil the vermicelli *al dente* (see page 24) and drain well. Serve with the shrimp mixture poured over, and garnished with the chopped coriander.

Peking Noodles with Shrimp

Peking noodles usually denotes a dish of flat noodles with a very pungent pork sauce. Here, however, the same sauce lightened a bit does very well with shrimp.

**5 dried mushrooms,* soaked in water for 30
minutes, soaking liquid reserved
2 tablespoons plus 2 teaspoons sesame oil ***
3 tablespoons hoisin sauce *
2 tablespoons soy sauce *
1 clove garlic, finely minced
2 tablespoons peanut oil
**½ pound medium raw shrimp, peeled, deveined,
and cut in half**
**1 teaspoon sherry or liquid from the dried
mushrooms**
**1 pound fresh Chinese noodles * or 1 pound
linguine**
**6 scallions, both green parts and white, cleaned
and chopped**

Slice the mushrooms into thin strips, then set aside in the
soaking liquid.

Combine the 2 teaspoons sesame oil, the hoisin sauce,
soy sauce, and garlic. Set aside.

Heat the oil in a wok or heavy skillet over a high flame. Add shrimp and stir-fry briefly, until the shrimp turn pink. Drain the mushrooms, reserving the soaking liquid, and add to the wok, then add the reserved sesame oil—hoisin sauce mixture, and sherry or mushroom liquid. Cook over reduced heat for about 2 minutes and set aside.

In a large kettle of boiling water, cook the noodles for 5 minutes if fresh or until tender if dried. Drain well and toss with the 2 tablespoons sesame oil in a serving bowl. Toss with the shrimp mixture, garnish with the chopped scallions, and serve immediately.

Chinese Browned Noodles with Shrimp

I like the taste of double-cooked noodles: first boiled, then fried in a little oil to brown around the edges, a favorite Chinese method that would translate well to other kinds of noodles.

5 dried mushrooms *
1 cup boiling water
4 ounces fresh mushrooms, sliced
7 tablespoons corn or peanut oil
½ pound medium raw shrimp, shelled and deveined
Salt to taste
2 tablespoons plus 2 teaspoons cornstarch
1 tablespoon soy sauce *
1 teaspoon granulated sugar
8 to 12 ounces fresh Chinese noodles * or linguine
½ cup chopped scallion green
1 cup chicken broth or mushroom liquid

Soak dried mushrooms in the boiling water for 15 to 30 minutes. Squeeze dry, reserving the soaking liquid.

Sauté the fresh mushrooms in 2 tablespoons of the corn oil until browned, then set aside.

Split the shrimp by slicing almost through ("butter-flying"). Salt, then toss lightly with the 2 teaspoons corn-starch and refrigerate for 30 minutes.

Combine the 2 tablespoons cornstarch, soy sauce, and sugar and set aside.

Boil the noodles for 4 or 5 minutes. Drain immediately in a colander, then run cold water through the noodles until cool. Set aside.

Put 2 tablespoons of the corn oil in a wok and heat. Stir-fry the shrimp until pink, then toss with sesame oil and the fresh and dried mushrooms and scallion green and set aside. Wipe out the wok with paper towels.

Heat the remaining 3 tablespoons corn oil in the wok. Add the noodles and flatten into a "pancake" over very high heat. Press down with a spatula as it browns and turn once to brown the other side.

In a skillet, heat the shrimp mixture over a high flame, adding the broth or mushroom liquid mixed with the re-served cornstarch mixture. Stir well.

Place the noodles on a platter, top with the shrimp mix-ture, and serve immediately.

Mee Krob (Thai Rice Stick with Pork and Shrimp)

This Thai dish has many interesting contrasts—the crisp, light fried noodles and rich smooth sauce, the nearly cloy-ing hoisin sauce "cut" by lemon peel, the contrasting

textures of fresh bean sprouts, pork, and shrimp. This is
an impressive dish to serve.

**Corn oil for deep frying, mixed with 1 tablespoon
sesame oil ***
**2 eggs, beaten with ¼ teaspoon cayenne pepper
and ½ teaspoon salt**
**¾ pound rice stick noodles,* pulled apart into 3-
or 4-inch one-layered sections**
2 tablespoons peanut oil
2 onions, finely chopped
3 cloves garlic, finely chopped
**1 pound pork tenderloin, sliced into paper-thin
pieces 2 inches long**
½ pound shrimp peeled and deveined
¼ cup hoisin sauce *
2 tablespoons tomato paste
¼ cup granulated sugar
3 tablespoons fish sauce *
1 tablespoon slivered lemon peel
Juice of 1 lemon
2 cups fresh bean sprouts, washed and drained
3 fresh green chilies, sliced very thin
**8 scallions, cut into 4-inch sections, both ends
fringed by cutting through with a sharp knife
and placed in ice water to curl**

Heat the corn and sesame oils together in large skillet or
wok to 325 degrees on a deep-frying thermometer. Let
the egg fall through a slotted spoon to form lacy pancakes
on the surface of the oil. Fry until brown, then turn and
brown other side. (The total cooking time will be less than
1 minute.) Drain on paper towels. Repeat until egg is
used up.

Raise the heat to 375 degrees. Drop in one piece of rice
stick at a time; it will swell and brown. Turn and brown
the other side, then drain on paper towels. Repeat with the

remaining rice sticks. Remove the oil and clean out the wok.

Add the peanut oil to the wok and heat. Add the onion, garlic, shrimp, pork, hoisin sauce, tomato paste, sugar and fish sauce and cook until thick, about 20 minutes, over medium heat. Add the lemon peel and juice.

Toss the shrimp mixture with half the rice stick noodles and place in a large serving bowl. Pile the rest of the noodles on top in a conical mound, spread the egg "lace" around sides, and arrange the bean sprouts as a "fringe." Scatter the chili shreds over all and garnish with the curled scallions, arranged like spokes around the cone.

Noodles with Scallops, Broccoli, and Mushrooms

Scallops and broccoli contrast interestingly in color, texture, and taste if you are careful not to overcook the broccoli. Serve with soy sauce if you like, but it is actually unnecessary, for the simple contrasts should be preserved without the binding and masking functions of a strong sauce.

1 head broccoli, separated into florets
2 tablespoons peanut oil
1 tablespoon finely chopped fresh ginger *
1 teaspoon finely chopped garlic
½ pound scallops, cut up if large
6 dried mushrooms,* soaked in warm water for
20 minutes, squeezed dry, and sliced
1 teaspoon salt
1 pound fresh Chinese noodles * or linguine

Cook the broccoli until barely tender, then drain well and set aside.

Heat the peanut oil in a heavy skillet or wok and add the ginger and garlic. Stir-fry until golden, then add the scallops and stir-fry for 2 minutes. Add the broccoli, mushrooms, and salt and stir-fry quickly for 2 minutes longer.

Boil the noodles *al dente* (see page 24). Drain well and let dry a few minutes, spread out on platter, then add to the wok and brown over high heat, tossing with the scallop mixture. Serve at once, with soy sauce, if desired.

Kung Pao Squid with Linguine

Kung Pao is a style of Chinese cooking, hot and garlicky and rich with bean paste, which is often used with shrimp. We are adapting this for use with squid, which is a delicious substitute.

2 pounds squid
2 tablespoons rice wine vinegar*
Salt to taste
1 teaspoon chili paste with garlic *
1 tablespoon hoisin sauce *
1 tablespoon bean paste *
2 tablespoons soy sauce *
4 teaspoons granulated sugar
4 cloves garlic, finely minced
2 tablespoons chopped scallions
2 tablespoons finely chopped fresh ginger *
2 tablespoons peanut oil
1 pound fresh Chinese noodles * or linguine

Clean the squid by pulling out the "head" and insides. Remove the hard cartilage, then carefully peel off the very thin purple skin. Cut into 2-inch squares, rinse, and pat dry.

In a mixing bowl, combine the vinegar, salt, chili paste with garlic, hoisin sauce, bean paste, soy sauce, and sugar. In another bowl, combine the garlic, scallions, and ginger.

Heat the peanut oil in a wok. Add the squid and stir-fry until curled and white. Add the ginger-garlic-scallion mixture and stir-fry for 2 minutes, then add the vinegar mixture and stir until it comes to a simmer.

Meanwhile, boil the noodles *al dente* (see page 24) and drain well. Pour the squid sauce over the noodles and serve immediately.

Khanom Jeen Nam Prik

This Thai dish, another contribution of Mrs. Puntipa Rajadhon of Bangkok, uses an assortment of seafood. Use whatever is seasonal and fresh. This is a "wet" noodle dish, and should be served in large soup bowls.

5 cloves garlic, chopped
2 tablespoons peanut oil
½ pound pork, thinly sliced
2 cups chicken or clam broth
2 tablespoons light soy sauce *
3 dried red chilies,* pounded
½ pound raw shrimps, peeled and deveined
1 tablespoon sesame oil *
1 pound thin egg noodles
At least 6 each freshly scrubbed mussels and clams
1 tablespoon lemon juice

½ cup chopped scallions
1 cup fresh bean sprouts
¼ cup chopped, dry-roasted peanuts

In a saucepan, sauté the garlic briefly in the peanut oil. Add the pork and stir-fry briefly, until it changes color. Add the chicken or clam broth and soy sauce, then bring to a boil and add the chilies, shrimps, and sesame oil.

Meanwhile, boil the noodles *al dente,* (see page 24), then drain and place in a serving bowl. Keep warm.

Add the clams and mussels to the mixture in the saucepan and simmer, covered, until their shells open. Add the lemon juice and scallions and remove from the heat. Stir in the bean sprouts and pour over the noodles. Garnish with the roasted peanuts and serve immediately.

Burmese Noodles with Shrimp Tok (Ground Shrimp and Spicy Salad)

This is another adaptation of Lorna Chin's recipe for shrimp *tok,* which she serves over a "pickled" vegetable salad. The method of preparing shrimp is very interesting. You could use these strips in a clear broth with seaweed as a Japanese-style Burmese soup.

¾ pound raw shrimps, peeled, deveined, and put through a meat grinder
3 tablespoons sesame oil
3 tablespoons peanut oil
1 cup shredded, seeded cucumber
2 cups shredded Chinese cabbage *
1 carrot, scraped and shredded

3 scallions, shredded
2 tablespoons soy sauce *
Salt and freshly ground black pepper to taste
1 teaspoon finely minced fresh ginger *
½ teaspoon crushed dried red chilies *
1 pound thin egg noodles
Chopped fresh green chilies for garnish

Shape the shrimp meat into flat patties. Combine 1 table-spoon of the sesame oil and the peanut oil and heat in a wok. Fry the shrimp patties over very high heat until browned and cooked through. Drain on paper towels, then, when cooled, slice into ½-inch slices.

Combine the cucumber, cabbage, carrot, scallions, soy sauce, salt and pepper, 1 tablespoon of the sesame oil, ginger, and crushed red chilies to make a salad. Set aside.

Boil the egg noodles *al dente* (see page 24), then drain well and toss with the remaining sesame oil. Set aside to cool to room temperature, tossing occasionally, then place on a serving platter and spread the salad on top. Arrange the shrimp-patty shreds on top of the salad, then serve, garnished with the chopped green chilies.

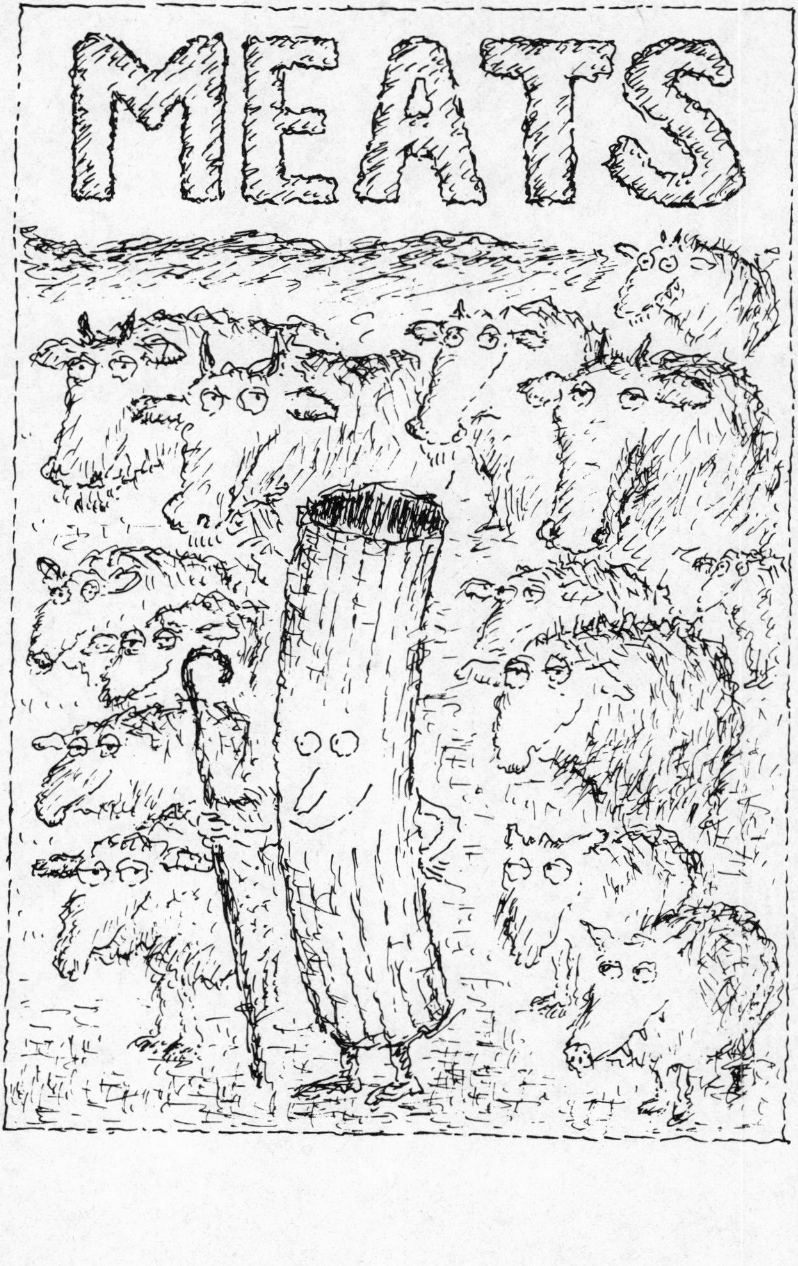

Meats

Eggplant-Meat Casserole with Noodles

Eggplant and ground beef combine well here, and in dishes like moussaka. The hard-boiled egg addition is true to southern Italian tradition.

Salt
1 medium eggplant, peeled and sliced
8 ounces macaroni
6 tablespoons olive oil, or as needed
Freshly ground black pepper to taste
1 pound lean ground beef
2 hard-boiled eggs, diced
½ pound mozzarella, thinly sliced
¼ cup freshly grated Parmesan cheese
2 tablespoons butter

Preheat the oven to 350 degrees.

Salt the eggplant slices and place in a colander to drain for 30 minutes. Pat dry with paper towels.

Boil the macaroni *al dente* (see page 24) and drain well.

Heat the olive oil in a skillet. Brown the eggplant, a few slices at a time, and toss with salt and pepper. Add more oil as needed. Remove the eggplant to another dish.

Add the beef to the skillet and sauté, stirring, until

broken up and browned. Off the heat, stir in the eggs and more salt and pepper.

In a buttered casserole, layer the noodles, eggplant, meat, and mozzarella, ending with a layer of eggplant. Top with the Parmesan, dot with the butter, and bake for 40 minutes.

Lentil Beef with Pasta

This is a good, hearty dish, rather like the lentil version of *pasta e fagioli,* but richer for the addition of stew meat. And, like all stews, best made a day ahead (except, of course, for the macaroni).

2 tablespoons olive oil
2 pounds chuck, cut into 1-inch cubes
4 onions, finely chopped
2 cloves garlic, finely minced
3 cups beef stock
Salt and freshly ground black pepper to taste
½ teaspoon dried oregano
½ teaspoon dried basil
1 cup red lentils, soaked in water for 2 hours
8 ounces macaroni

Heat the oil in a heavy casserole. Brown the beef and onion in it, then add the garlic, stock, salt and pepper, oregano, and basil. Partially cover and cook for 45 minutes to 1 hour.

Add the lentils, drained, and cook for 30 minutes more, or until the beef and lentils are tender.

Meanwhile, cook the macaroni *al dente* (see page 24) and drain well. Place the macaroni in a serving bowl and pour the meat and lentils over it.

Red, White, and Green Pasta

This is an attractive, Italian-flag-colored dish, with a spicy, smoky taste from the bacon and peperoni. Full of spirit.

1 pound farfalle or gemelli
6 slices bacon, cut into 1-inch pieces
4 slices peperoni, in shreds
6 ounces fresh mushrooms, sliced
3 tomatoes, peeled, seeded, and chopped (see page 51)
1 large scallion, chopped
Salt and freshly ground black pepper to taste

Cook the pasta *al dente* (see page 24) and drain well.

Sauté the bacon until crisp in a heavy skillet. Pour out all but 2 tablespoons of the fat, then add the peperoni and sauté briefly. Add the mushrooms and sauté, stirring, for 5 minutes, or until wilted; add the tomatoes and simmer just until soft. Season with salt and pepper and toss with the pasta and scallions, then serve, with freshly grated Parmesan cheese on the side.

Prosciutto and Tomatoes with Vermicelli

Prosciutto deserves center stage once in a while, and when it does, as in this recipe, or in fettucine tossed with cream, it should be good, imported prosciutto. You can cheat elsewhere.

2 tablespoons butter
6 ounces prosciutto, cut into thin slivers
4 medium tomatoes, peeled, seeded, and chopped
(see page 51)
1 cup chicken stock
Salt and freshly ground black pepper to taste
1 pound vermicelli
2 tablespoons chopped chives

Heat the butter in a saucepan and sauté the prosciutto over low heat. Add the tomatoes, chicken stock, and salt and pepper and simmer for about 15 minutes, allowing the liquid to reduce a little.

Boil the vermicelli *al dente* (see page 24) and drain well. Toss with the sauce, garnish with the chives, and serve.

Rotini with Sausages, Peperoni, and Navy Beans

This is your basic beans and sausages, enlivened by a spicy and rich tomato sauce and served over whatever interesting pasta you like. Rotini or penne would be good here.

2 tablespoons olive oil
2 onions, finely chopped
2 cloves garlic, finely chopped
1 large fresh green chili, finely chopped
1 pound fresh Italian pork sausages, sliced
1 peperoni, thinly sliced
1 can (35 ounces) Italian tomatoes in puree,
roughly chopped
1 can (20 ounces) navy beans, drained and rinsed

**1 tablespoon chopped fresh basil or 1 teaspoon
dried
1 teaspoon granulated sugar
Salt and freshly ground black pepper to taste
½ cup freshly grated Parmesan cheese
1 pound rotini**

Preheat the oven to 350 degrees.

Sauté the onion in the oil until golden. Add the garlic
and fresh chili and sauté for 5 minutes, then add the pork
sausages and peperoni and sauté for 5 minutes longer. Add
the tomatoes, navy beans, and seasonings.

Boil the rotini *al dente* (see page 24). Drain well and toss
with the sauce, then place in a casserole and top with the
grated cheese. Bake for 45 minutes.

Green and White Noodles with
Ham and Mushrooms

My brother, Henry Isaacs, first served us this elegant dish.
Like other fettucine and prosciutto combinations, it de-
pends for its success on freshly made noodles (bought or
homemade), good prosciutto, and last-minute assemblage.

**1 pound fresh mushrooms, chopped
3 scallions or 2 shallots, finely chopped
6 tablespoons butter
Salt and freshly ground pepper to taste
6 ounces prosciutto, julienned
1 cup heavy cream
8 ounces each fresh green spinach noodles, and
fresh white noodles (fettucine), either homemade
(see pages 19–21) or factory bought
½ cup freshly grated Romano cheese
Fresh parsley for garnish**

Heat half the butter in a heavy skillet. Add the scallions
and mushrooms and stir over medium-high heat until the
mushrooms give off their juices. Add salt and pepper to
taste, then turn down the heat and add the prosciutto. Set
aside.

Boil two pots of water, one for each kind of pasta. Cook
until *al dente* (see page 24) and drain well.

Meanwhile, place the remaining butter in a heatproof
serving dish and warm it in a low oven. Put the noodles
in the dish, then toss with the cream. Add the ham and
mushroom mixture. Top with the Romano, garnish with
parsley, and serve immediately.

Linguine Carbonara

Carbonara is an Italian classic. It is delicious, and ex-
tremely quick and easy to prepare. Some recipes have you
leave all the bacon fat in; I remove most of it.

1 tablespoon olive oil
1 medium onion, minced
¾ pound bacon, minced
1 pound linguine
2 eggs
**2 tablespoons freshly grated Romano pecorino
cheese**
Salt and freshly ground black pepper to taste
Snipped chives for garnish

Heat the oil in a skillet and sauté the onion until golden.
Add the bacon and sauté until just done, not crisp. Drain
off all but 2 tablespoons of the fat.

Meanwhile, bring a large kettle of water to a boil and start cooking the linguine. While the linguine is cooking, beat the eggs and cheese together. Set aside. Drain the linguine and put in a serving dish.

Add salt and pepper to the bacon mixture and stir. (If there is more than ¾ tablespoon of oil and fat in the skillet, drain some off.) Add the egg mixture to the skillet and stir well, adding salt if needed. Toss with the linguine, garnish with the chives, and serve at once.

Pasta with Beans and Sausage

This is one of the first dishes I ever made as an adult (I don't count childhood fudge making), and it goes through transformations constantly. Different sorts of beans, sausages, and shapes of pasta appear in it, rarely ones that don't go quite well with each other. If there is time, I use dried beans cooked *al dente*. Canned beans are often mushy.

2 medium onions
½ pound linguica, chorizo, or other sausage
1 can (20 ounces) white kidney beans
2 pounds tomatoes
2 cloves garlic, diced or pressed
1 tablespoon chopped fresh basil or 1 teaspoon dried
½ teaspoon granulated sugar
Salt and freshly ground black pepper to taste
1 pound egg noodles
2 tablespoons butter
½ cup freshly grated Parmesan cheese

Sauté the onion and sausage in a casserole, then add the tomatoes, beans, garlic, basil, and seasonings and mix well. Cook over low heat for at least 40 minutes.

Boil the egg noodles *al dente* (see page 24), then drain and toss with the butter and cheese. Pour the sauce over and serve.

Linguine with Hot Italian Sausages and Basil Meatballs

Allowing myself only one Italian meatball and spaghetti recipe, I chose this one—a nearly perfect version of the dish. The meatballs, sausages, and sauce are also good baked in layers with lasagne noodles.

Meatballs

1 medium onion, finely chopped
2 cloves garlic, finely chopped
2 tablespoons olive oil
2 tablespoons freshly grated Parmesan or Romano cheese
1 ½ pounds ground beef and pork, mixed
3 slices white bread, soaked in ½ cup milk and squeezed dry
2 eggs
Salt and freshly ground black pepper
2 tablespoons finely chopped fresh basil or 1 tablespoon dried

Sauce

1 onion, finely chopped
2 cloves garlic, finely minced
2 tablespoons olive oil
1 can (16 ounces) tomato sauce
1 can (35 ounces) whole Italian plum tomatoes
1 can (6 ounces) tomato paste
1 tablespoon granulated sugar
Salt and freshly ground pepper to taste
1 tablespoon finely chopped fresh basil or 1½
teaspoons dried
1½ pounds hot Italian sausages, cut in 1-inch chunks,
sautéed until brown, and well drained
2 pounds linguine

Make the meatballs first. Sauté the onion and garlic in the 2 tablespoons oil until golden, then combine with all the other meatball ingredients. Knead the mixture until it is smooth and well blended, then make the walnut-sized meatballs and chill them on a platter for 30 minutes.

Meanwhile, make the sauce. Sauté the onion and garlic together in the oil in a heavy skillet. When golden, add all the other sauce ingredients except the sausages and simmer over very low heat for 30 minutes.

Sauté the meatballs, a few at a time, in a large skillet. As they brown and become firm, add them to the tomato sauce. Pour off the accumulated fat from the skillet, then sauté the sausages. Add them to sauce and let simmer for 30 minutes. Serve on the hot boiled linguine, cooked *al dente* (see page 24).

Vermicelli with Meat Sauce and Feta Cheese

Feta, with its dry sharpness, is an excellent foil to a hearty meat sauce. Serve right after you add the feta to the sauce; you should be eating it as it begins to melt in.

1 medium onion, chopped
2 tablespoons olive oil
¾ pound ground beef
1 can (35 ounces) Italian plum tomatoes
1 can (6 ounces) tomato paste
Salt and freshly ground black pepper to taste
1 tablespoon granulated sugar
¼ cup chopped fresh basil or 2 tablespoons dried
6 ounces feta cheese
1 pound vermicelli
1 tablespoon butter

Sauté the onion in the olive oil over medium heat, then add the ground beef and sauté until meat is browned and broken up. Add the tomatoes and tomato paste. Mix well, then add the salt, pepper, sugar, and basil and let simmer. Add the cheese to the sauce just before serving.

Meanwhile, boil the vermicelli *al dente* (see page 24), then drain and mix with the butter in a serving bowl. Serve, topped with the sauce.

Pasta with Ground Beef Cooked in Wine

This beef sauce from Lombardy is aromatic with fennel. My friend Ruth Bell, who gave me this recipe, says it must be reheated the next day to take full advantage of the seasonings.

2 tablespoons butter
2 onions, finely chopped
1½ pounds ground beef
Salt and freshly ground black pepper to taste
Pinch of freshly grated nutmeg
3 bay leaves
1 chicken or beef bouillon cube
1 can (35 ounces) Italian plum tomatoes
¾ cup dry red wine
1½ tablespoons fennel seeds, tied in cheesecloth
1 pound spaghetti

Heat the butter in a skillet and sauté the onion until golden. Add the beef and stir until browned and broken up, then add the remaining ingredients (except the spaghetti) and simmer for 30 to 45 minutes (in Italy it is left to cook at the back of the stove overnight). Remove the bag of fennel seeds, then refrigerate until serving time.

Boil the spaghetti *al dente* (see page 24), then drain well and serve with the sauce, reheated, and freshly grated Parmesan cheese.

Bahmie Goreng (Indonesian Fried Noodles)

These fried noodles contain a number of fascinations of mine, including fish sauce and dried mushrooms. The way the pork is treated in this dish is particularly appealing, and the final assemblage is an orgy of tastes.

**4 large dried mushrooms,* soaked in boiling
water for 15 minutes, soaking liquid reserved
1 tablespoon dark soy sauce *
1 teaspoon molasses
¾ pound boneless pork tenderloin
1 pound fresh Chinese noodles * or linguine
¼ cup peanut oil
1 large onion, cut in thin slivers
1 cup Chinese cabbage,* shredded
1 clove garlic, minced
2 fresh green chilies, seeded and minced
½ pound medium raw shrimps, peeled and deveined
1 teaspoon fish sauce,* or to taste
2 tablespoons light soy sauce *
Chopped scallions for garnish**

Squeeze the mushrooms dry and slice, reserving the soaking liquid.

Combine the dark soy sauce and molasses in a glass or ceramic bowl and marinate the pork for 1 hour, then roast the pork in a small pan, with the marinade, for 45 minutes. Cool and cut in strips.

Boil the noodles *al dente* (see page 24), then drain and toss with 1 tablespoon of the peanut oil.

In a wok or large skillet, heat the remaining oil and sauté the onion, cabbage, garlic, and fresh chilies for 2 minutes. Add the shrimp and stir-fry for 3 minutes more, then add the noodles, pork, light soy sauce, fish sauce, and reserved mushroom liquid. Stir until heated through, then place in a serving dish and garnish with the scallions.

Gudyo Pat

Thai noodle dishes can be very complex, like *pathai* (see page 138), or quite simple. A friend, Jane Siegel, had this often when she lived in Bangkok, and says that it has all the basic tastes of Thai food except the spicy heat. You can use chicken or shrimp instead of pork, or for that matter parboiled vegetables.

1 pound wide, flat egg noodles
3 tablespoons peanut oil, or as needed
8 cloves garlic, peeled and chopped
¼ pound pork, thinly shredded
1 teaspoon fish sauce,* or to taste
1 teaspoon granulated sugar
2 tablespoons soy sauce *
3 scallions, chopped

Cook the noodles *al dente* (see page 24), then drain them and dry them on paper towels.

Fry the chopped garlic in peanut oil until brown, then add the pork shreds and cook until brown as well.

Add the noodles and fry until lightly browned, then add the fish sauce, sugar, and soy sauce and heat through. Garnish with the scallions and serve.

Thai "Wet" and "Dry" Noodles

Like other Thai and Southeast Asian noodle dishes, this one is served either "wet," soupy with broth, or "dry," as a noodle garnish. This method of double-cooking pork is very common in Chinese cooking as well.

½ pound pork tenderloin, fat removed
2 tablespoons peanut oil
3 cloves garlic, peeled and thinly sliced
2 fresh green chilies, seeded and finely chopped
½ teaspoon crushed dried red chilies *
Fish sauce * to taste
1 teaspoon granulated sugar
Vinegar to taste
½ cup dry-roasted peanuts
4 scallions, chopped
½ cup chopped fresh coriander
Bean sprouts, washed and picked over (optional)
4 cups chicken or other broth (for "wet"— optional)
1 pound narrow, flat noodles, like linguine

Boil the pork until cooked through, about 20 minutes, then drain and slice thin. Set aside.

Heat the peanut oil in a wok and fry the garlic until golden. Add the sliced pork, fresh and dried chilies, fish sauce, sugar, and vinegar. Cook briefly, stirring.

Meanwhile, boil the noodles *al dente* (see page 24). Drain and place in individual bowls. Add the meat mixture to each bowl, then garnish with the peanuts, scallions, coriander, and bean sprouts.

Or, if "wet," heat the chicken or other broth and pour over the noodles before adding the garnishes.

Spicy Lamb with Vermicelli

This is a simple, Hunam-style recipe: it should be *hot*. You could serve the lamb pieces over soaked, instead of fried, bean thread noodles.

1 pound lean lamb, boned
2 teaspoons salt
2 teaspoons cornstarch
½ teaspoon granulated sugar
1 cup peanut oil
2 tablespoons hoisin sauce *
1 tablespoon minced fresh ginger *
1 teaspoon finely minced garlic
2 tablespoons soy sauce *
Hot chili oil * or Tabasco to taste
3 packages (2 ounces each) bean thread noodles *

Cut the lamb into thin shreds and mix with the salt, cornstarch, and sugar. Heat the oil in a wok and deep-fry the lamb until browned, then remove with a slotted spoon and drain on paper towels.

Heat the oil again and separate the noodles into small handfuls. Fry each handful quickly, for about 2 seconds, and drain well.

Remove all but 2 tablespoons of the oil and heat. Stir-fry the ginger and garlic briefly, then add the soy sauce, hoisin sauce, and hot chili oil or Tabasco. Place the noodles in a bowl, top with the lamb, and pour the sauce over. Toss and serve.

Peking Noodles

Peking noodles was the dish that first introduced me to northern Chinese cooking, and I feel quite sentimental about it. It is also invariably appetizing and quite filling.

1 tablespoon peanut oil
½ pound ground beef
3 cloves garlic, finely minced
2 tablespoons dry sherry
½ cup finely chopped scallions
3 tablespoons hoisin sauce *
2 tablespoons soy sauce *
1 teaspoon vinegar
½ cup water
1 pound linguine or fresh Chinese noodles *
1 cucumber, peeled, sliced in half,
seeded, and shredded, for garnish
½ pound bean sprouts, washed and picked over,
for garnish
2 scallions, chopped, for garnish

Heat the oil in a wok, then stir-fry beef and garlic until both are browned and the beef is broken up. Pour off all but about 2 tablespoons of the fat. Add the sherry, scallions, hoisin sauce, soy sauce, and vinegar and let simmer. Add the ½ cup water and bring back to a simmer.

Meanwhile, boil the noodles *al dente* (see page 24) and drain well. Serve with the sauce on top and the garnishes on the side.

Noodles with Ma Po Bean Curd

Ma Po is my favorite style of bean curd. It is a hot, peppery pork sauce with lumps of bean curd in it, subtly flavored with perfumy, smoky Szechuan brown peppercorns. Served with noodles, it is a filling meal.

5 squares fresh bean curd *
½ pound ground pork
1 tablespoon finely chopped garlic
3 scallions, finely chopped
1 tablespoon chili paste with garlic *
2 tablespoons soy sauce *
1 teaspoon salt
1 cup water or stock
1 teaspoon Szechuan brown peppercorns,*
pulverized in a mortar
1 pound fresh Chinese noodles * or linguine
2 teaspoons cornstarch mixed with 2 teaspoons
cold water
1 tablespoon sesame oil *

Cut the bean curd into ½-inch cubes and set aside.

In a dry, heavy skillet or wok, fry the ground pork over high heat, stirring to separate as it browns. Add the garlic, scallions, chili paste with garlic, soy sauce, salt, stock or water, pepper, and bean curd and bring to a simmer. Simmer for about 10 minutes.

Meanwhile, boil the noodles *al dente* (see page 24), then drain well and place in a serving bowl.

Add the cornstarch mixture to the bean curd mixture and stir very gently, over medium heat, until the mixture thickens. Sprinkle with the sesame oil and serve, tossed with the noodles.

Sha-Cha Beef Noodles

Friends who have lived in Taiwan remember making this, or often buying bowls of it late at night from noodle stalls, where it is made to order. This is only one version of the dish, and this one has its own variations: you can make it "dry" or "wet" with beef broth. The "barbecue sauce" that is called for is *nothing* like our barbecue sauces, so don't use them. Chinese bottled "barbecue sauce" is made from sesame oil and dried shrimp, among other things.

½ pound lean beef, in shreds
2 tablespoons cornstarch
½ teaspoon salt
Pinch of granulated sugar
2 tablespoons soy sauce *
1 pound fresh Chinese noodles * or linguine
2 tablespoons peanut oil, more if necessary
2 cups washed, shredded mustard greens, Chinese cabbage,* or regular cabbage
4 scallions, chopped
2 tablespoons "barbecue sauce" *
4 cups hot beef broth (for "wet"—optional) mixed with 1 tablespoon soy sauce
2 tablespoons chopped scallions for garnish

Combine the beef with the cornstarch, salt, sugar, and the soy sauce in a small bowl. Set aside.

Cook the noodles *al dente* (see page 24), then drain well.

Heat the peanut oil in a wok or heavy skillet and fry the beef mixture in it for about 2 minutes, stirring. Remove the beef with a slotted spoon and set aside.

Add more oil if necessary, then add the greens and stir-fry over high heat. Add the scallions and stir-fry briefly, then add the "barbecue sauce" and stir for 1 minute.

Place noodles in individual bowls and top with the meat and vegetables. (If the "wet" version is desired, pour the beef broth and soy sauce mixture over the noodles.) Garnish with the chopped scallion and serve.

Thopa (Tibetan Noodle Dish)

In Tibet, noodles are a staple food. I learned this recipe from Pasang Sherpa in Kathmandu, a man who makes a fine muscatel wine, and who, is I think, a true Renaissance man. Noodles are often used in ceremonial occasions, like the mid-winter "noodle day" on which the Gu-thu is eaten. On the twenty-ninth day of the twelfth month a special form of noodles is made, the Gu-thu, into which are put stones, a piece of wood, wool, and other things, all wrapped in dough. When the bowls of noodles are served, one opens one's dough lump and the item one receives is an indication of one's fortune. One of them means that the recipient has to provide barley beer for all the rest. Traditionally, one eats nine bowls of this, and there are chants to go with the bowls, such as "Having eaten the Gu-thu who cares if one is ill! Having eaten the Gu-thu who cares if one dies!"

½ **pound lean beef, very thinly shredded**
2 **cloves garlic, minced**
2 **tablespoons peanut oil**
5 **fresh red or green chilies, finely chopped**
6 **to 8 scallions, cut into 2-inch thin shreds 2**
inches long
2 **tablespoons shredded fresh ginger** *
2 **medium carrots, scraped and cut into shreds 2**
inches long
5 **cups beef or chicken broth**
1 **green pepper, seeded and shredded**
Salt to taste
1 **pound thin egg noodles**

Combine the beef shreds with the garlic. Heat the oil in a heavy skillet and stir-fry the beef shreds quickly until brown, then add half the chilies, half the scallions, and half the ginger and stir-fry for 2 minutes. Add the carrots and stir-fry for 2 minutes more.

Bring the broth to a simmer in another pan and add the remaining chilies and ginger, the shredded green pepper, and salt to taste.

Meanwhile, boil the egg noodles *al dente* (see page 24). Drain, then divide between soup bowls. Add some of the meat mixture to each, pour the broth over, and garnish with the remaining scallions. Serve immediately.

Stir-fried Bean Curd Noodles

When a friend told me a bean curd factory had just opened in Boston's Chinatown, I went to get some of the firm, silky soy cakes. The "factory" is a long basement room, five steps down from street level, with a steamy soy atmosphere. The family—mother, father, grown son, and grandmother—do all the work, stirring the soy mash in large cauldrons, letting it firm into cakes in wooden frames. But the nicest surprises of all are the by-products of bean curd making, such as soy milk; soy custard, which is delicious with honey (it is rather like yogurt); and bean curd noodles. These are fresh, thickish strips of curd that has been dried slightly. Rinsed, patted dry and stir-fried with meat and vegetables, they are unusual and delicious.

3 tablespoons peanut oil
3 Chinese sausages * or pork or beef in shreds
2 scallions, cleaned and chopped
1 tablespoon finely minced fresh ginger *
1 green pepper, thinly sliced in strips
3 tablespoons soy sauce *
1 cup chicken broth *
1 ½ pounds bean curd noodles
1 tablespoon cornstarch mixed with ¼ cup cold water
1 tablespoon sesame oil *

Heat 1 tablespoon of the peanut oil in a heavy skillet or wok. Stir-fry the sausages or meat until brown, then add the scallions, ginger, and green pepper and stir-fry for 2 minutes. Add the soy sauce and chicken broth and bring to a boil. Reduce the heat to very low.

Meanwhile, wash and drain noodles well. Heat the remaining oil in another skillet or wok and stir-fry the noodles until lightly browned.

Add cornstarch mixture to the sauce and stir quickly until thickened. Toss with noodles and serve sprinkled with the sesame oil.

Soba with Chinese Sausages, Peas, and Mushrooms

This is an invention combining a love of Japanese *soba* noodles and Chinese pork sausages. The slightly sweet broth mixture is also "Japanese." A very aesthetic dish— dark reddish sausages, light green peas, and black mushrooms against pale green noodles.

1 pound *soba* noodles *
1 bag *dashi* *
2 cups water
10 dried mushrooms, soaked in hot water for 30 minutes, soaking liquid reserved
3 Chinese sausages,* sliced and steamed for 5 minutes
2 tablespoons soy sauce *
1 tablespoon finely minced fresh ginger *
1 teaspoon salt
1 teaspoon granulated sugar
1 cup frozen peas
3 scallions, chopped

Boil the *soba* noodles *al dente* (see page 24) and drain well.

Put the *dashi* bag in the boiling water and simmer for 20 minutes, then add the mushrooms, reserved mushroom liquid, and sausages and cook at a simmer for 2 minutes. Add the soy sauce, ginger, salt, and sugar, then add the peas and cook for 4 minutes. Place the *soba* noodles in a serving bowl and pour the sausage mixture over. Garnish with the scallions and serve.

Egg Vermicelli and Sausages

One of the basic noodle-cooking methods in Asia involves precooking the noodles and then frying them over high heat with quick-cooking ingredients, until they are browned and crisp in places. Like fried rice, this dish has a last minute, "scrambled" egg addition.

¾ pound thin egg vermicelli (see note below)
3 eggs
1 tablespoon soy sauce *
1 teaspoon sesame oil *
3 tablespoons peanut oil
3 thinly sliced Chinese sausages *
1 tablespoon finely minced fresh ginger *
½ teaspoon granulated sugar
Salt to taste
3 scallions, chopped

Boil the noodles *al dente*. (These take only a few minutes —sometimes only 4.) Drain well.

Beat the eggs with the soy sauce and sesame oil. Set aside.

Heat the peanut oil in a wok or heavy skillet. Sauté the sausages and ginger for 2 minutes, stirring, then add the drained noodles and stir-fry until they brown in places. Add the sugar, salt, and scallions and then, stirring, the egg mixture. Stir-fry until eggs are cooked. Serve at once.

Note: Philippino grocers have some called "angel's hair," in skeins.

Spinach and Pork with Noodles

Spinach and pork are an excellent noodle combination. This recipe is quite simple, and exploits the flavors well.

1 tablespoon dry sherry
2 tablespoons soy sauce *
1 teaspoon granulated sugar
1 teaspoon salt
½ pound pork tenderloin, in shreds
8 dried mushrooms *
2 tablespoons peanut oil
1 package (10 ounces) fresh spinach, washed and picked over
2 scallions, chopped
1 pound fresh Chinese noodles * or spaghetti
2 teaspoons sesame oil *

Combine the sherry, soy sauce, sugar, and salt in a bowl and add the pork shreds. Let marinate for 1 hour.

Soak the dried mushrooms in warm water for 20 minutes, then squeeze dry and slice.

Heat the peanut oil in a wok or heavy skillet and stir-fry the pork and mushrooms for 5 minutes. Add the spinach and scallions, then cover and let cook over high heat, just until the spinach is wilted.

Meanwhile, boil the noodles *al dente* (see page 24), then drain well and toss with sesame oil. Serve immediately, tossed with the pork and spinach mixture.

Kuksoo Bibim I

Korean noodle dishes are very delicious, and there are many variations on the basic garlic, sesame, and chili combination of seasonings. Here are two versions, ground pork and shredded beef, of the classic bean thread noodle dish.

½ **pound bean thread noodles** *
½ **pound ground pork**
3 **tablespoons soy sauce** *
2 **teaspoons granulated sugar**
2 **tablespoons chopped scallions**
3 **cloves garlic, minced**
4 **teaspoons sesame seeds**
1 **tablespoon sesame oil** *
3 **cucumbers, peeled, cut in half lengthwise, and seeded**
½ **teaspoon salt**
1½ **tablespoons peanut oil**
1 **scallion, minced**
Cayenne pepper to taste
2 **eggs, beaten**
1 **cup beef bouillon**

Boil the noodles for 3 or 4 minutes, then drain them well. Cool with cold water and drain again.

Heat a wok or heavy skillet and stir-fry the pork, separating it as it browns. Add 2 tablespoons of the soy sauce, the sugar, chopped scallions, and minced garlic. Stir in 2 teaspoons of the sesame seeds, crushed in a mortar, and the sesame oil and set aside.

Cut the cucumbers into long thin pieces, then into 2-inch lengths, and add salt. Heat 1 tablespoon of the peanut oil in another skillet. Add the cucumbers and stir-fry briefly with the minced scallion, remaining sesame seeds, cayenne, and remaining tablespoon soy sauce. Remove from the heat.

In a flat frying pan, heat a little oil and fry the eggs into a pancake. Let cool, then cut into thin strips.

Reheat the pork mixture, add the bouillon, and bring to a simmer.

Place the noodles in individual bowls. Add some cucumber mixture to each, then meat mixture, and garnish with egg and more scallion.

Kuksoo Bibim II

This is the shredded beef version.

½ pound beef, in shreds
3 tablespoons soy sauce *
2 tablespoons sesame oil *
1½ tablespoons sesame seeds, crushed in a mortar
2 tablespoons granulated sugar
Salt and freshly ground black pepper
2 cloves garlic, minced
1 cucumber, peeled, cut in half lengthwise, and seeded
2 medium eggs
½ pound bean thread *

Mix the beef shreds with the soy sauce, sesame oil, sesame seeds, sugar, salt, pepper, and garlic. Heat in a wok or heavy skillet seasoned with 2 teaspoons of peanut oil.

Shred the cucumber into strips.

Beat the eggs lightly and fry into a pancake in a flat skillet, then cool and cut into narrow strips.

Combine the beef, cucumber, and eggs and set aside

while you boil the noodles *al dente* (see page 24). Drain and place in a bowl, then cover with the beef mixture and serve.

Chungking Pork with Noodles

Chungking pork, though not usually served with noodles, has a definite affinity for them. A common addition to this dish is salted, fermented black beans, rinsed, dried and *slightly* mashed.

½ pound lean pork
2 cups water
1 teaspoon dry sherry
2 tablespoons minced fresh ginger *
3 tablespoons peanut oil
3 cups sliced green cabbage
¼ cup bean paste *
3 tablespoons soy sauce *
2 teaspoons dried red chilies *
2 cloves garlic, minced
1 pound linguine or fresh Chinese noodles *

Simmer the pork in a small saucepan with the 2 cups water, sherry, and 1 tablespoon of the minced ginger until tender. Let the pork cool in the saucepan, then cut into large slices. Reserve the cooking liquids.

Place half the peanut oil in a wok or saucepan over medium heat. Then add the cabbage and stir-fry for about 1 minute, or until partially translucent. Remove and set aside.

Add the remaining peanut oil to the wok or saucepan, then add the bean paste, soy sauce, dried red chilies, garlic, pork, and pork stock. Cook, stirring, for another minute.

Meanwhile, cook the noodles *al dente* (see page 24) and drain well.

Return the cabbage to the pork mixture, pour the sauce over the noodles, and serve immediately.

Stir-fried Noodles with Chinese Sausage and Dried Shrimp

Chinese pork and liver sausages, the small, hard ones, have become a staple in my house. They have a subtle anise flavor—a kind of Chinese peperoni—and are not too spicy. They keep in the refrigerator for weeks, freeze well, and are delicious wherever you include them. Dried shrimp, with their interesting fishiness, are a great foil for them.

1 pound fresh Chinese noodles * or linguine
2 tablespoons sesame oil *
1 cup dried shrimp *
4 Chinese sausages
2 tablespoons peanut oil
½ cup chopped scallions
3 tablespoons soy sauce *

Parboil fresh noodles for 5 minutes, then drain, toss with the sesame oil, and set aside. (If you are not using fresh noodles, boil dried ones just *al dente* and drain well.)

Soak the dried shrimp in water for about 1 hour.

Slice the sausages and steam in a colander or vegetable steamer basket for 5 minutes over boiling water. (This removes extra fat.)

In a wok or heavy skillet, heat the peanut oil. Add the

noodles and stir-fry over high heat until the noodles begin to brown. Add the drained shrimp, scallions, sausages, and soy sauce and stir over medium heat until heated through. Serve immediately.

Kung Lo Mein, Burmese Style

Burmese food has recently caught my fancy, due to the excellent cooking of Mrs. Lorna Chin of the Mandalay Restaurant in Boston. This is not her recipe, however, but my adaptation of a dish I ate in the Chins' restaurant.

1 teaspoon sesame oil *
¼ cup peanut oil
8 cloves garlic, peeled and sliced
½ pound duck, pork, or chicken meat, cooked and cut into small cubes
2 cups shredded Chinese cabbage *
8 ounces spinach, shredded
3 scallions, chopped
3 fresh green chilies, seeded and finely chopped
1 pound fresh Chinese noodles * or linguine

Heat the oils in a wok until very hot. Drop in the garlic pieces and fry them until brown; *do not let them burn.* Remove with a slotted spoon and drain on paper towels.

Remove all but 2 tablespoons of oil from the wok. Heat, add the meat, and stir-fry until browned. Reduce the heat and add the cabbage, spinach, scallions, and chilies and stir-fry for 2 minutes, or until the spinach wilts.

Boil the noodles *al dente* (see page 24), then drain and toss with the meat and vegetable mixture. Sprinkle with the crisp garlic bits and serve.

Pork and Bean Sprout Lo Mein

A well-made lo mein dish, with fresh ingredients and as-sembled at the last minute, is a treat. The twice-cooked noodles with their crisp, brown edges are splendid tossed with crisp sautéed vegetables. Nothing like the versions served in "greasy chopstick" places.

½ pound pork tenderloin, in shreds
1 tablespoon cornstarch
1 tablespoon soy sauce
1 pound thin fresh Chinese noodles * or linguine
Sesame oil *
2 tablespoons peanut oil
1 cup bamboo shoots,* julienned
2 cups bean sprouts, washed and picked over
1 teaspoon salt
½ cup chopped scallions
2 tablespoons finely chopped fresh coriander
or flat parsley

Combine the pork with the cornstarch and soy sauce. Set aside.

Boil the noodles *al dente* (see page 24), then drain well in a colander and run cold water over them. Place in a bowl and toss with 1 tablespoon sesame oil. Set aside.

In a large wok or skillet, heat the peanut oil. Add the pork and stir-fry over high heat for 2 minutes, until the shreds separate and are browned. Add the bamboo shoots, lower the heat to medium, and stir-fry for 1 minute. Add the noo-dles and raise the heat, tossing the mixture often until some of the noodles are browned and they are all heated through.

Add the bean sprouts and stir-fry for 2 minutes. Add the salt and toss, then add the scallions, fresh coriander or parsley, and sesame oil to taste and toss well. Serve immediately.

Meat Kreplach

Even if one has one's grandmother's recipe for these, they never have quite the same taste. These come close to my grandmother's, and perhaps to yours. Like wonton, like *tortellini* and ravioli, these are a staple of sorts, and can be served a number of different ways: baked as an appetizer or with a light tomato sauce, or, best of all, I think, floating in a perfect chicken broth.

Noodle Dough

2 eggs
½ teaspoon salt
2 cups all-purpose flour
½ eggshell water

Meat Filling

2 tablespoons rendered chicken fat
1 small onion, finely chopped
1 pound ground lean beef
Salt and freshly ground pepper to taste
1 egg

To make the noodle dough, beat the eggs in a bowl and add the salt, flour, and water. Knead until smooth and elastic, adding more flour is necessary. Form into a ball and set aside, covered with a clean cloth, for 30 minutes.

For the filling, heat the chicken fat in a small skillet and sauté the onion until golden. Add the meat and cook, stirring to separate it, until it is brown. Add salt and pepper and remove from the heat. Let cool, then beat in the egg.

To form the kreplach, roll the dough out on a floured board or tabletop until very thin. Cut into 2-inch squares and place a teaspoonful of meat mixture on each square. Fold the dough over the meat to form a triangle and pinch the edges together hard, moistening with water if needed to make a good seal. Press the two corners at the base of the triangle together and set aside on a towel.

Cook the kreplach in boiling salted water for about 20 minutes before adding to soup, or before sautéing in peanut oil, or baking.

Hungarian Layered Noodles

A version of this dish was made for us in London. The long baking merges the flavors nicely. Every time we make this, it turns out differently, depending on the sausages available, what cheeses we use, and so forth. Always delicious, and a fine winter supper.

3 medium potatoes, peeled and cut in chunks
½ pound (2 sticks) butter, melted
8 ounces large macaroni, shells or ziti, boiled
al dente
6 hard-boiled eggs, quartered

½ pound bacon, sautéed until crisp and drained
½ pound pancetta or other cured ham, sliced
1 pound hot Italian sausages, cut into chunks
1 pint commercial sour cream
1 cup freshly grated Gruyère cheese
Salt and freshly ground black pepper to taste
½ cup bread crumbs

Boil the potatoes in salted water just until tender, then drain and toss with 2 tablespoons of the butter.

Boil the pasta *al dente* (see page 24), then drain and toss with 2 tablespoons of the butter.

Preheat the oven to 325 degrees.

In a buttered casserole, layer the potatoes, eggs, noodles bacon, ham, sausages, sour cream, and cheese. Salt and pepper to taste, using plenty of pepper. Top with bread crumbs and pour the remaining butter over all, then bake for 2 hours, or until bubbly—keep the heat low; it should take at least 1½ hours to get browned.

Portuguese Marinated Pork and Clam Sauce with Linguine

Marinating pork in wine and herbs makes it a different sort of animal. This preparation is often used in "mock" game recipes. Here, with clams, it is a very interesting sauce for linguine.

1 pound boneless pork, cut in thin strips 2 inches long
½ cup dry white wine
2 cloves garlic, peeled and crushed
Salt and freshly ground pepper to taste

1 teaspoon chopped fresh thyme or ½ teaspoon
dried
½ teaspoon cayenne pepper
2 tablespoons peanut oil
1 pound littleneck clams, scrubbed
1 pound linguine

Marinate the pork strips in the wine, garlic, salt and pepper, thyme, and cayenne. Set aside for 2 or 3 hours in the
refrigerator.

Drain the pork, reserving the marinade, then pat dry
with paper towels. Heat the oil in a heavy saucepan and
sauté the pork until well browned. Add the reserved marinade and cover. Simmer for 20 minutes, then add the clams
and cover. Cook until the clams open, about 10 minutes.

Meanwhile, boil the linguine *al dente* (see page 24)
and drain well. Toss with butter, then top with the pork
and clams, arranging clams on top and pouring the sauce
over them.

Tanzanian Pork and Plantain Noodles

Plantains are used in much Caribbean and African cooking,
and are worth experimenting with. They are available in
many city markets. Try them baked, sautéed, or in this
African curry.

6 plantains or greenish bananas
3 tablespoons peanut oil
1 large onion, finely chopped
1 pound pork tenderloin, in 1-inch chunks

**2 large tomatoes, peeled, seeded, and chopped
(see page 51)
2 large green peppers, seeded and chopped
1 tablespoon imported curry powder, preferably
Madras ***
**2 cups water
Salt and freshly ground pepper to taste
1 pound string beans, ends removed and broken
into 2-inch pieces
1 pound broad egg noodles**

Skin and slice the plantains or bananas and place in a
bowl with water to cover (to keep from browning).

Heat oil in a large, heavy saucepan. Add the pork and
onions and brown, stirring. Add the tomatoes, green peppers, curry powder and the 2 cups of water. Simmer for
30 minutes, then add salt and pepper to taste, the bananas, and the string beans. Simmer for 15 minutes or more,
until the vegetables are done.

Boil the noodles *al dente* (see page 24), then drain.
Pour the sauce over to serve.

Bassi (Ethiopian Beef and Squash Sauce for Noodles)

Yellow summer squash and beef in a spicy, peanutty sauce
may be a little strange to our tastes, but it is a delicious
concoction. Ethiopian stews, like Nigerian and some other
African dishes, use peanuts both as a thickener and as a
source of protein. With beans, beef, peanuts, and noodles,
this dish is as protein-rich as you could want.

2 tablespoons peanut oil
2 medium onions, chopped
2 cloves garlic, finely minced
1 pound boneless beef, in 1-inch chunks
2 tablespoons tomato paste
1 can (20 ounce size) haricot or white pea beans or
1½ cups dried beans, soaked overnight and cooked
until tender
1 large green pepper or sweet red pepper, seeded
and diced
1 cup peanut butter
Tabasco to taste
½ pound summer squash, in 2-inch cubes
Salt and freshly ground pepper to taste
1 pound broad egg noodles

In a heavy kettle, heat the oil and sauté the onion and garlic. Add the beef and sauté for about 3 minutes, until the color changes. Add the tomato paste, beans, and green pepper, then add water to cover the ingredients and simmer, uncovered, for 40 minutes. Let the sauce reduce to about 2 cups.

Mix the peanut butter and Tabasco with a little water to thin. Add, along with the squash and salt and pepper, to the mixture in the kettle. Simmer for 15 minutes more, or until the beef is tender.

Meanwhile, boil the noodles *al dente* (see page 24). Drain well, then pour the sauce over and serve.

Tunisian Lamb Balls with Noodles

Tunisian lamb recipes, like Persian meat dishes, often include a fruit. Apricot sauce may seem a doubtful ingredient, but it is perfectly suited to this dish.

2 medium onions
1 pound lamb, minced
1 tablespoon finely chopped fresh mint or 1
teaspoon dried
½ teaspoon ground cumin
1 tablespoon minced fresh parsley
Salt and freshly ground black pepper to taste
1 egg
All-purpose flour for coating
3 tablespoons peanut oil
2 tablespoons butter
1 small jar apricot jam, heated and sieved
3 tablespoons lemon juice
1 pound very thin egg noodles

Put the onions and lamb through a meat grinder, then combine with the mint, cumin, parsley, salt, pepper, and egg. Knead well, then form into small balls and roll in flour to coat.

Heat the oil and butter to bubbling in a heavy skillet and brown the meatballs well.

Combine the apricot jam and lemon juice in a small saucepan and heat to a simmer.

Cook the noodles *al dente* (see page 24), then drain and place in a serving dish. Arrange the meatballs on the noodles, then top with the apricot sauce and serve.

Pork and String Bean Goulash
with Noodles

Pork, sour cream and crisp sautéed string beans make a delicious sauce for noodles. Marinating the pork in vinegar (you could use dry white wine) is a trick I learned from

the Portuguese dish of marinated pork and clams on
page 189.

1 pound pork tenderloin, in ½-inch cubes
2 tablespoons white wine vinegar
3 cloves garlic, finely minced
½ teaspoon dried thyme
Salt and freshly ground black pepper to taste
2 tablespoons butter
¾ pound fresh string beans, ends removed and
broken into 1-inch pieces
2 tablespoons olive oil
3 medium onions, thinly sliced
1 tablespoon imported Hungarian paprika
¼ cup dry white wine
¾ pound macaroni (gemelli, for example)
½ pint commercial sour cream
¼ cup chopped chives

Place the pork in a glass or glazed bowl and add the vinegar, garlic, thyme, salt, and pepper. Set aside for 1 hour.

In a large skillet, heat the butter and sauté the string
beans over high heat, until spottily browned—less than 5
minutes.

In another skillet, heat the oil and sauté the onions
slowly, until browned and soft. Add the paprika and salt
and pepper to the onions, then add the pork. Raise the
heat, stirring, to boil off the liquid and brown.

Add the white wine and simmer until the pork is tender, then reduce the heat and toss in the string beans.

Meanwhile, boil the macaroni *al dente* (see page 24)
and drain.

Add the sour cream to the pork and beans and stir well.
Season to taste, then serve over the noodles, garnished with
chives.

Espagueti con Salchichas

This is a Caribbean/Spanish version of spaghetti with sausages, made more lively with chilies, olives, and capers. The sauce is best when made the day before serving, and a teaspoon or so of fresh lemon juice helps too.

2 tablespoons peanut oil or margarine
1 tablespoon salt pork, finely chopped
¼ cup ham, roughly chopped
1 medium onion, finely chopped
1 medium tomato, roughly chopped
1 green pepper, seeded and chopped
3 small fresh green chilies, seeded and chopped
8 green olives, pitted and chopped
1 teaspoon capers
½ pound garlic sausage or hot Italian pork sausage
1 can (8 ounces) tomato sauce
1 pound medium spaghetti

Heat the oil or margarine in a heavy saucepan and brown salt pork and ham for about 3 minutes. Add the onion, tomato, green pepper, fresh chilies, olives, and capers and cook slowly for 5 minutes, then cut the sausage into small chunks and add, along with the tomato sauce. Cook for 5 minutes longer, stirring.

Meanwhile, boil the spaghetti *al dente* (see page 24). Drain well and serve with the sauce and freshly grated Parmesan cheese.

Chili with Macaroni

Chili with macaroni is an old standby, but no less delicious and welcome for that. You can assemble this, based on a recipe by Joy Walker, and refrigerate or freeze before baking.

2 tablespoons olive oil
3 medium onions, chopped
1 pound ground beef
2 stalks celery, chopped
2 green peppers, seeded and chopped
Oregano, chili powder, and thyme or savory to
taste
1 teaspoon granulated sugar
1 can (35 ounces) Italian plum tomatoes, roughly
chopped
2 cans (20 ounce size) red kidney beans,
drained
1 pound small macaroni
3 tablespoons chopped fresh coriander

Heat the oil in a heavy kettle. Sauté the onions until browned, then add the beef, breaking up the lumps as it browns. Add the celery, green peppers, oregano, chili powder, thyme or savory, sugar, and tomatoes. Cook for about 20 minutes, then add the kidney beans and cook for 10 minutes longer.

Preheat the oven to 350 degrees.

Boil the macaroni *al dente* (see page 24) and drain well. Toss with the chili mixture, place in a buttered casserole, and bake for 40 minutes.

Macarrones con Costillitas de Cerdo

Like the Caribbean spaghetti with sausages, this dish contains olives and capers, which distinguishes it from a plain tomato sauce. A messy dish to eat, for you must negotiate the bones of the spareribs. Large cloth napkins are a necessity.

2 tablespoons margarine creamed with 1 teaspoon Hungarian paprika
½ cup chopped smoked ham
1 tablespoon finely chopped salt pork
1 green pepper, seeded and chopped
1 onion, finely chopped
1 can (8 ounces) tomato sauce
2 pounds spareribs, cut into ribs and chopped in half
1 tablespoon plus 1 teaspoon salt
½ cup pitted black olives
1 tablespoon drained capers
1 cup water
1 pound elbow macaroni
1 tablespoon olive oil
1 can (20 ounces) Italian plum tomatoes
½ cup freshly grated Parmesan cheese

Heat the margarine in a large, heavy saucepan. Add the ham, salt pork, green pepper, and onion and sauté quickly until the onion is browned. Add the tomato sauce, spareribs, 1 teaspoon salt, olives, capers, and water, then cover and simmer for 40 minutes, adding more water if necessary.

Meanwhile, cook the macaroni *al dente* (see page 24) in boiling water to which has been added the olive oil and the 1 tablespoon salt. Drain well.

Add the whole tomatoes and macaroni to the sauce and cook, covered, for 15 minutes. Then toss with the cheese and serve.

Calves' Liver Smetana

However enlightened and, perhaps, impoverished we become, we still don't use innards enough. This is a Hungarian recipe for which you can substitute chicken livers just as well.

¾ pound calves' liver, partly frozen, sliced very thin
2 tablespoons all-purpose flour, seasoned with salt and freshly ground black pepper to taste
1 medium onion, finely chopped
5 slices bacon
1 teaspoon dried thyme
1 pound medium egg noodles
½ pint commercial sour cream
Chopped fresh parsley for garnish

Sauté the bacon until crisp in a heavy skillet. Drain on paper towels, then pour off all but 2 tablespoons of the fat from the skillet.

Sauté the onion in the bacon fat until golden, then add the calves' liver, first dredged in the seasoned flour, and toss for 5 minutes, until cooked through. Crumble the bacon in, then add the thyme and more salt and pepper to taste. Remove from the heat.

Boil noodles *al dente* (see page 24), then drain and place in a serving bowl.

Reheat the liver mixture briefly. Add the sour cream and blend well, taking care not to let the mixture boil. Pour over the noodles and toss, then serve, garnished with parsley.

Pastitsio

Pastitsio is a Greek version of baked macaroni and beef casserole. The white sauce topping is different, however, and reminiscent of the topping for moussaka, and the addition of cinnamon and nutmeg to the meat mixture is a hint of Middle Eastern influence.

2 tablespoons butter
2 tablespoons olive oil
1 large onion, chopped
½ pound ground beef
½ pound ground lamb
½ cup dry white wine
½ cup tomato sauce
3 tablespoons tomato paste
2 cloves garlic, finely chopped
½ teaspoon ground cinnamon
1 teaspoon dried oregano
¼ teaspoon freshly grated nutmeg
Salt and freshly ground black pepper to taste
3 medium tomatoes, peeled, seeded, and roughly chopped (see page 51)
½ cup fresh bread crumbs
1 pound macaroni
¾ cup freshly grated Parmesan cheese
2 cups White Sauce (page 267)
2 cups Tomato Paste Sauce (page 265)

In a large skillet, heat the butter and oil together and cook the onion until golden. Add the ground beef and lamb and cook, stirring to break up lumps, until browned. Pour off any extra fat, then add the wine, tomato sauce, tomato paste, garlic, cinnamon, oregano, nutmeg, salt, pepper, and tomatoes and simmer for 10 minutes, or until thick, over low heat. Stir in the bread crumbs and set aside.

Preheat the oven to 400 degrees.

Boil macaroni *al dente* (see page 24) and drain. Put half the macaroni into a buttered casserole and sprinkle on ¼ cup of the Parmesan. Add all the meat sauce and cover with the remaining macaroni. Sprinkle on another ¼ cup Parmesan, then cover with the white sauce and sprinkle with the remaining Parmesan. Bake for 35 minutes or until browned, then cut into squares and serve with the homemade tomato sauce.

Veal Paprikash

Hungarian goulashes and other meat stews with sour cream are best served with the slightly curly, flat egg noodles. An alternative method of preparation involves marinating the veal for an hour in the wine, herbs, onions, and garlic before browning it.

4 tablespoons (½ stick) butter
2 onions, minced
4 cloves garlic, finely minced
2 pounds veal stew meat, in 1-inch chunks
1 bay leaf
1 teaspoon dried thyme
1 cup dry white wine
Salt and freshly ground black pepper to taste
3 tablespoons sweet Hungarian paprika

2 teaspoons tomato paste
1 pint commercial sour cream, at room
temperature
½ cup chopped fresh dill or 1 tablespoon dried dill
weed
1 pound curly egg noodles

Heat 2 tablespoons of the butter in a heavy saucepan. Add
the onion and garlic and stir over medium heat until
browned, then add the veal and stir while browning. Add
the bay leaf, thyme, wine, salt, pepper, and paprika and
bring to a simmer. Stir in the tomato paste, add water if
necessary to cover the meat, and cover the pan. Cook over
low heat until the meat is tender, about 30 or 40 minutes.

Boil the egg noodles *al dente* (see page 24), then drain
and toss with the remaining butter. Stir the sour cream and
dill into the stew and serve over the noodles.

POULTRY

Poultry

Chicken Liver Sauce for Egg Noodles

The simplest possible sauce—and quite luxurious tasting. Use good sherry or Marsala. It will be obvious if you haven't. This is also good (and traditional) with gnocchi.

1 pound chicken livers
All-purpose flour, seasoned with salt and freshly
ground black pepper to taste
3 tablespoons butter
½ cup dry sherry or Marsala
¾ cup heavy cream
1 pound egg noodles
2 tablespoons chopped fresh parsley

Cut the chicken livers into chunks and dredge with the seasoned flour. Heat the butter to bubbling in a skillet and sauté the chicken livers briefly. Add the sherry or Marsala, then reduce the liquid over medium-high heat for 3 minutes.

Boil the noodles *al dente* (see page 24) and drain.

Add the heavy cream to the sauce and bring to a boil rapidly. Boil for 2 minutes, then add salt and pepper to taste and pour over the noodles. Garnish with the parsley and serve.

Turkey Noodle Casserole

A hearty and simple dish, excellent for leftover turkey. A sort of country cousin to Tetrazzini.

2 tablespoons butter
1 tablespoon vegetable oil
1 medium onion, finely chopped
1 clove garlic, minced
1 pound egg noodles, boiled *al dente* (see page 24) and drained well
1 pound cooked dark-meat turkey, in 1-inch chunks
Salt and freshly ground black pepper to taste
Brown Sauce (see below)
½ cup bread crumbs mixed with ¼ cup freshly grated Parmesan cheese

Preheat the oven to 325 degrees.

Heat the butter and oil in a heavy skillet and sauté the onion and garlic until golden. Toss this mixture with the cooked noodles and place in the bottom of a buttered casserole. Add the turkey chunks and salt and pepper to taste, then add brown sauce and top with the bread crumbs and Parmesan.

Bake until bubbly and browned, 30 to 45 minutes.

Brown Sauce

1 small onion, minced
1 tablespoon butter
2 tablespoons all-purpose flour
2½ cups beef or turkey stock
½ teaspoon dried thyme
½ cup dry white wine
Salt and freshly ground black pepper to taste

Sauté the onion in the butter until deep brown. Add the flour and cook, stirring, for 2 minutes, then add the beef or turkey stock, thyme, and white wine. Stir as it comes to a boil and begins to thicken, then let it simmer for 20 minutes. Season to taste with salt and pepper; you will have about 2 cups of sauce.

Turkey Tetrazzini

This is an elegant version of an old standby that is excellent for buffets. It can be frozen or refrigerated before baking.

8 ounces spaghetti
8 tablespoons (1 stick) butter or margarine
3 tablespoons minced fresh shallots
Salt and freshly ground black pepper to taste
½ pound fresh mushrooms, sliced
3 cups cooked, cubed turkey
¼ cup all-purpose flour
2 cups turkey or chicken broth
½ cup heavy cream
¼ cup dry sherry
2 egg yolks
¼ cup freshly grated Parmesan mixed with ¼ cup bread crumbs

Boil the spaghetti *al dente* (see page 24) and drain well. Toss with 2 tablespoons of the butter or margarine and set aside.

Heat 3 tablespoons of the butter or margarine in a skillet and sauté the shallots for 3 minutes, stirring. Add salt and pepper and mushrooms and sauté briefly, until the mushrooms wilt. Place the mixture in a bowl and add the turkey.

In a saucepan, melt the remaining butter or margarine and stir in the flour. Cook, stirring, for a few minutes; do not allow to color. Add the broth gradually, whisking to keep the mixture smooth, and cook until thick. Simmer gently for 5 minutes, then add salt and pepper to taste. Combine the cream, sherry, and egg yolks in a bowl and gradually whisk in some of the hot sauce. Return the contents of bowl to the saucepan and heat gently, stirring, over very low heat for a minute. Taste for seasoning, then combine the sauce with the turkey mixture.

Preheat the oven to 350 degrees.

Place the spaghetti in a buttered 2-quart casserole. Make a hole in the center and pour in the turkey mixture, then sprinkle the cheese and bread crumb mixture over and bake for about 45 minutes, or until browned and bubbly.

Chicken and Peanuts with Noodles

Chicken with all sorts of nuts—almonds, cashews, and especially peanuts—is a feature of Chinese cooking. Be careful when roasting the nuts, because they burn or get dark and bitter very easily.

1 pound boned, skinned chicken meat, in 1-inch chunks
3 tablespoons peanut oil
4 ounces shelled raw peanuts
½ cup chopped scallions
¼ cup hoisin sauce *

1 tablespoon rice wine vinegar *
2 teaspoons dry sherry
1 teaspoon granulated sugar
3 cloves garlic, minced
2 ½ teaspoons sesame oil *
¾ pound vermicelli or thin egg noodles

Sauté the chicken in 1 ½ tablespoons of the peanut oil until cooked through.

Place the peanuts on a baking sheet and brown in a 400-degree oven for about 5 minutes, then combine with the scallions, cooked chicken, hoisin sauce, rice vinegar, sherry, sugar, garlic, and ½ teaspoon of the sesame oil.

Cook the noodles until soft, then drain and add the remaining sesame oil.

Heat the remaining peanut oil in a wok over a very high

flame. Add the noodles and stir-fry for a few minutes, then add the chicken mixture, stir over high heat for another minute, and serve.

Whole-Wheat Noodles with Chicken

This eclectic, but delicious, recipe combines Chinese flavorings and Japanese fish/seaweed broth with whole wheat noodles, which you can find in most health food stores.

1½ pounds dark-meat chicken
1 tablespoon cornstarch
2 tablespoons peanut oil
¼ cup soy sauce *
1 tablespoon sesame oil *
1 tablespoon dry sherry
½ cup chopped scallions
Salt and freshly ground black pepper to taste
2 quarts water
1 bag *dashi* (Japanese soup stock) *
1 pound whole-wheat noodles

Skin and bone the chicken, then cut the meat into shreds. Mix the shreds with the cornstarch, then stir-fry, in the peanut oil, over high heat until cooked through. Add the soy sauce, sesame oil, sherry, scallions, and salt and pepper and stir-fry briefly. Set aside.

Meanwhile, bring the 2 quarts of water to boil in a large saucepan. Add the *dashi* bag and simmer for 20 minutes. At the same time, boil the whole-wheat noodles *al dente* (see page 24). Drain, then add to the stock along with the chicken mixture and serve.

Fried Thai Noodles

The addition of broccoli to the traditional Thai noodle dish improves it in both texture and color. You might try other vegetables as well.

1 pound wide, flat noodles
2 teaspoons sesame oil *
2 tablespoons peanut oil, more if necessary
2 cloves garlic, peeled and sliced
2 cups shredded, cooked chicken or shrimp
3 tablespoons bean paste *
2 tablespoons fish sauce,* or to taste
Salt and freshly ground black pepper to taste
2 cups broccoli florets
Chicken or beef stock as needed
Soy sauce * to taste
1 tablespoon rice wine vinegar *
1 teaspoon granulated sugar
1 tablespoon cornstarch mixed with 1 tablespoon
water

Boil the noodles *al dente* (see page 24), then drain, toss with the sesame oil, and cool.

Heat the oil in a wok. Add the cooled noodles and stir over high heat until browned. Place on a serving dish and keep warm.

Add more oil to wok, if needed, then add the garlic and stir-fry until golden. Add the chicken or shrimp and stir-fry briefly.

Add the bean paste, fish sauce, and salt and pepper, and toss broccoli in the mixture. Add just enough stock to cover, then bring to boil and cook until the broccoli is just tender.

Add the soy sauce, vinegar, and sugar and cook till heated through, then add the cornstarch mixture and stir over the heat until thick. Pour over the noodles and serve.

Cold Chicken and Celery with Soba

An adaptation of a cold Chinese chicken dish to Japanese *soba* noodles, also often served cold. I have also made this dish with farfalle (pasta in the shape of small bows), and it was quite elegant.

3 pounds chicken thighs and legs
½ cup chopped fresh ginger *
3 slivers lemon rind
1 pound *soba* noodles *
¼ cup sesame oil *
1 tablespoon sesame seeds, parched on a baking
sheet in a 400-degree oven for 5 minutes
3 cups julienned celery
¼ cup sesame paste *
2 tablespoons rice wine vinegar *
1 tablespoon light soy sauce *
1 tablespoon lemon juice
Tabasco to taste

Place chicken pieces in a kettle and add the ginger and lemon rind. Cover with cold water, then bring to a boil and simmer, covered, for 40 minutes. Let cool in the liquid.

Poach the julienned celery in boiling water for 2 minutes, then drain and chill.

Boil the *soba* noodles *al dente* (see page 24), then drain and toss with 2 tablespoons of the sesame oil and sesame seeds. Chill.

Bone and shred the chicken. Arrange chicken and celery over noodles, then combine the remaining ingredients including the rest of the sesame oil, and add to the noodle mixture just before serving.

Korean Cold Noodles

This is similar to the two Korean *kuksoo bibim* meat dishes (see pages 181–182), but served cold in a way that is good for summer. The cooled chicken broth should not have jelled: if it does jell, add just enough warm water, beating with a whisk, to liquefy it.

2 whole chicken breasts
¼ cup plus 1 teaspoon soy sauce *
**1 tablespoon chopped scallions, both green part
and white**
**1 tablespoon sesame seeds, toasted in a dry pan
and ground with mortar and pestle**
2 teaspoons sesame oil *
1 clove garlic, finely minced
Salt and freshly ground black pepper to taste
½ can (6 ounce size) Szechuan cabbage pickles
1 ½ teaspoons granulated sugar
2 eggs
1 pound *soba* noodles *
Cayenne pepper to taste

Skin the chicken breasts, then place in a saucepan and add enough water to cover. Bring to a boil and simmer for 15 or 20 minutes, or until just cooked through. Cool in the liquid for 1 hour, then remove; reserve the liquid, letting it cool.

Bone the chicken, then cut the meat into thin strips, or pull apart with the fingers. Combine with 2 tablespoons of the soy sauce, the scallions, sesame seeds, 1 teaspoon of the sesame oil, the garlic, salt, pepper, Szechuan pickle, and 1 teaspoon of the sugar and set aside.

Beat the eggs together with the 1 teaspoon soy sauce, ½ teaspoon sugar and salt to taste. Make "pancakes" in an oiled, heated skillet; don't let them brown. Cool and slice into thin strips.

In a large kettle of boiling water, cook the noodles *al dente* (see page 24). Drain immediately, run cold water over them, and drain again. After cooling the noodles, toss them with the remaining soy sauce, sesame oil, and sugar and cayenne pepper.

Chill. Just before serving, divide the noodles among 6 serving bowls and top with the chicken mixture. Pour the reserved (cooled) liquid over the noodles to fill the bowls, and garnish with egg pancake strips.

Malay Chicken with Vermicelli

A third-hand recipe that comes to me from Judith Strauch, who learned it herself in Malaysia from an Indian cook. The curry powder is not packaged, but made up from an assortment of cumin, coriander, chilies, fenugreek, turmeric, and fennel seeds—in unmeasured proportions. My own mixture involves these ingredients in the following proportions:

2 ounces coriander seeds
2 ounces cumin seeds
4 to 6 dried red chilies
2 ounces ground turmeric
½ ounce ground cinnamon
¼ ounce ground cloves
2 ounces ground fenugreek
Seeds from 3 cardomom pods, pounded in a mortar

All of the above—heated until the mixture is aromatic in a dry heavy skillet, and ground in a mortar or in a blender until pulverized—can be kept for a week or so, tightly

covered, without losing much flavor. It is best to grind the
mixture just before you need it, however.

5 tablespoons clarified butter
5 large onions, diced fine and then mashed or
put in the blender
4 medium tomatoes, peeled and cut in small
pieces (see page 51)
1 small chicken, boned and meat cut in small
pieces
1 tablespoon salt
1 tablespoon chili powder
5 cloves garlic, diced fine and then mashed or put
in the blender
1 tablespoon finely diced fresh ginger *
2 tablespoons (or more to taste) of the spice
mixture (see above)
Juice of 1 lime
¾ cup water
1 pound vermicelli
Parsley or fresh coriander leaves for garnish

Heat the butter in a large, heavy saucepan. Add the mashed
onion and sauté, stirring, until browned. Add the tomatoes
and fry for 1 minute, stirring well, then add the chicken
and stir-fry for 2 minutes, until the meat becomes firm.

Add the salt, chili powder, garlic, ginger, and spice mixture and stir. Add a little water and stir as mixture cooks
over low heat, for about 10 minutes. Add the lime juice
and ¾ cup water and let boil for about 5 minutes.

Boil the noodles *al dente* (see page 24) and drain well.
Toss the chicken mixture with the noodles, garnish with
the parsley or coriander, and serve immediately.

Dick Chen's Szechuan Noodles

Mr. Chen teaches Chinese cooking in Montreal, where he has developed this version of a well-known dish. He provides two sauces, one tossed with the noodles, one used as a dipping sauce.

Noodle Mixture

**12 ounces spaghetti
1 whole chicken breast
1 tablespoon peanut oil
1 teaspoon sesame oil ***
2 tablespoons Szechuan preserved vegetable,*
diced

Sauce I

**1 ½ tablespoons peanut oil
½ teaspoon chili paste with garlic ***
**1 rounded tablespoon peanut butter
½ teaspoon sesame oil ***

Sauce II

3 tablespoons soy sauce *
2 tablespoons white wine vinegar *
**1 pinch salt
1 tablespoon sesame oil ***

Throw the spaghetti into boiling water. When it rises to the top, add 1 cup cold water; when it rises again, add another cup cold water. At the third rise, drain the noodles and let them cool in a container of cold water. Taste; they should be done.

Place the chicken breast in cold water in a saucepan

and bring to a boil. Let simmer for 5 to 8 minutes, or until cooked through. Remove and cool.

Place the drained noodles in a large bowl and toss with the peanut oil, sesame oil, and Szechuan preserved vegetable. Skin the chicken and pull into shreds. Place on top of the noodles.

For Sauce I, place the peanut oil, chili paste, and peanut butter in a cold wok and turn the heat on to high. Reduce to medium, then stir in the sesame oil. Stir-fry for 2 minutes, then pour over the noodles and chicken. Toss.

For Sauce II, combine the ingredients and serve with noodles.

Chinese Hot Pot

An absorbing dish to eat, with no advance work besides the cutting up and arrangement of ingredients. Like the Japanese *mizutaki,* hot pot, or hor gwo, is a diner participation dish in which each person picks out morsels from a central simmering broth. In some versions each person selects raw ingredients from a platter and holds them in the broth while they cook. In Singapore, Chinese restaurants set up tables on the sidewalks, each with a simmering pot in the center, into which skewers of fish, chicken, meat, and vegetables are dumped to cook. In all versions, diners have dipping sauces for their food, and, when all is cooked and eaten, the noodles and broth are poured into each person's bowl as a last "course." For the cooking utensil you can use a Chinese hot pot, which has a central chimney using hot coals and a moat around it for the simmering broth, or an electric skillet or any electric casserole you can place in the center of a table and maintain at a simmer.

Broth

2 quarts chicken broth, approximately
2 thin slices fresh ginger *
1 teaspoon sesame oil *
½ teaspoon salt

Hot Pot Ingredients

½ pound raw chicken, beef, or lamb, thinly sliced
½ pound raw sea bass or other firm fish; and/or
shrimp, peeled and deveined; or scallops and
squid, cleaned, sliced, and parboiled; or ¼ pound
baby beef liver
1 can Chinese fishballs,* drained
1 pad fresh bean curd * cubed
2 eggs, beaten with ½ teaspoon soy sauce and ½
teaspoon sugar, then fried without browning in a
"pancake," cooled, and cut into slices
2 cups shredded lettuce
1 cup shredded raw spinach
1 cup fresh bean sprouts
1 cup watercress leaves
¼ pound fresh mushrooms, sliced
6 dried mushrooms,* soaked in warm water, for
15 minutes, then drained and sliced
1 jar hard-boiled quail eggs,* drained
1 bunch scallions, sliced
2 bunches cellophane noodles * or 1 package very
fine Chinese egg noodles,* both soaked in warm
water

Dipping Sauce

Soy sauce
Chili paste with garlic
Rice wine vinegar *
Sesame paste * or *tahini*
Granulated sugar

Arrange all the ingredients on platters or in sections of the cooking utensil. In the latter case, simply pour the broth—which has been heated with the ginger, sesame oil, and salt for 10 minutes and strained—into the pot over the ingredients. Keep at a simmer for a few minutes before eating.

If a more leisurely version is desired, heat the broth with the ginger, sesame oil, and salt and have each diner choose his ingredients and cook them. Each guest can make a dipping sauce by combining the soy sauce, chili paste with garlic, vinegar, sugar, and sesame paste to taste, and dip each cooked ingredient before eating.

When everyone is done eating, add the noodles to the broth and heat through. Serve the broth and noodles to each diner.

Mizutaki

Mizutaki is the Japanese version of the Chinese hot pot (see page 218 for directions). The Japanese version tends to be simpler, and the big difference is in the dipping sauce. The Chinese dip is spicy and oily, while the Japanese is strong with biting horseradish and tangy with lemon.

Hot Pot Ingredients

**2 quarts clear chicken broth
1 small chicken, boned and cut into chunks; or
½ chicken and ¾ pound firm white fish in small chunks; or all fish
2 pads bean curd,* in 1-inch cubes
4 large dried mushrooms,* soaked in warm water for 15 minutes, then drained and sliced**

1 small head Chinese cabbage,* shredded
8 scallions, shredded
3 carrots, scraped and cut into thin slices on a
slant
2 small bundles *shirataki* noodles,* soaked and
drained

Sauce I

1 small *daikon* (long white horseradish), grated
½ teaspoon *wasabi* powder *
¼ cup Japanese soy sauce *
1 teaspoon lemon juice

Sauce II

Lemon juice mixed with soy sauce, to taste

Arrange all ingredients to be cooked on a serving tray.

Heat the broth in a cooking pot or an electric skillet in the middle of the table. Add salt to taste.

Each diner cooks ingredients as wanted for 2 minutes or so, and then dips in sauce before eating.

When all the meat, fish, and vegetables are eaten, add the noodles to the pot and raise heat. Cook for 2 minutes, then divide the soup and noodles among the diners' bowls.

Chili Chicken with Noodles

Chinese quick-cooked dishes are very popular in Indian cities, and are often adapted to Indian tastes, like the following "chili chicken," which is a version of a recent recipe directed to Delhi housewives.

1 small chicken or 2 whole chicken breasts, boned and cut into 1-inch chunks
2 teaspoons salt
¼ teaspoon cayenne pepper
½ teaspoon freshly ground black pepper
1 egg white
2 tablespoons cornstarch
½ cup peanut oil
1 large onion, chopped
6 cloves garlic, finely chopped
6 fresh green chilies, seeded, peeled, and finely chopped
2 tablespoons finely chopped fresh ginger *
8 large, fresh mushrooms, sliced
1 large cucumber, peeled, seeded, and cut into 1-inch cubes
1 tablespoon vinegar

1 tablespoon soy sauce *
1 teaspoon granulated sugar
1 pound linguine, boiled *al dente* (see page 24)
and drained

Combine the chicken chunks with 1 teaspoon of the salt, the cayenne and black peppers, egg white, and cornstarch.

Heat the peanut oil in a skillet and fry the chicken, a few pieces at a time, until all are done. Remove the chicken and all but 2 tablespoons of the oil from the skillet.

Reheat the oil and stir-fry the onion, garlic, chilies, and ginger for 3 minutes. Add the mushrooms and cucumber and stir for 1 minute more, then add the chicken and heat through. Add the remaining teaspoon salt, the vinegar, sugar, and soy sauce.

Serve over the linguine.

Noodles with Curried Chicken

Though my own invention, this dish is closest to a Southeast Asian noodle curry, for the method of cooking is similar to Chinese stir-frying while the ingredients are "Indian." If you cannot find raw cashews (try health food stores), use dry-roasted ones.

1 tablespoon mustard oil or corn oil
1 onion, finely chopped
1 tablespoon finely chopped fresh ginger
1 teaspoon each fennel seeds, cumin, coriander, and turmeric, ground or pounded with a mortar and pestle
2 small dried red chilies, pounded
3 chicken leg quarters, boned and sliced into 2-inch-long shreds
1 cup water, more if necessary
1 tablespoon cornstarch mixed with 2 tablespoons water
1 pound vermicelli or very thin egg noodles
Large handful raw cashews
2 tablespoons chopped parsley or fresh coriander

In large, heavy skillet, heat the oil until it smokes. Add the onion, then reduce the heat slightly to sauté until golden. Add the ginger and cook, stirring, for 2 minutes. Add all the spices and cook, stirring, for a minute longer.

Add the chicken and cook, stirring, until the shreds separate, then add about 1 cup of water and stir until it comes to a boil. Lower the heat to a simmer and cover the skillet. Let cook for about 15 minutes. (If the water has boiled away in that time, then add another cupful. It should still be covering the chicken when it is done.)

Stir up the cornstarch mixture and add to the chicken, stirring as it cooks and thickens. Cover and keep warm while preparing the noodles.

In a large pot of boiling water, cook the vermicelli until just tender, about 5 to 7 minutes. Drain well and place in a serving bowl.

Add the raw cashews to the chicken and toss well, then put the chicken mixture in the center of the bed of noodles. Garnish the whole with the chopped parsley or coriander and serve.

Poule au Pot à la Crème

A *poule au pot,* or poached chicken, is excellent served on a bed of broad egg noodles to absorb the juices and bits of vegetables. Even better when, as in this recipe, the sauce is bound with thickened cream.

1 chicken, (4 pounds) left whole
3 tablespoons butter
1 tablespoon olive oil
3 carrots, scraped and sliced
2 turnips, peeled and sliced
3 medium onions, sliced
2 stalks celery, chopped
Salt and freshly ground black pepper to taste
½ teaspoon dried thyme
½ cup dry white wine or vermouth
1 bay leaf
2 cups water
1 pound broad egg noodles
1 cup heavy cream

In a heavy casserole, brown the chicken on all sides in 2 tablespoons of the butter and the oil. Add all the vegetables and sauté for 3 minutes, then add salt and pepper, the thyme, wine, and bay leaf and simmer for 2 minutes. Add the 2 cups of water and cover. Simmer for 1 hour or until the chicken is tender. Remove the chicken to a platter and keep warm.

Boil the noodles *al dente* (see page 24), then drain and toss with the remaining tablespoon of butter.

Meanwhile, raise the heat under the chicken cooking liquid and reduce it by one-half. Add the heavy cream and boil very quickly, stirring, until it begins to thicken slightly. Taste for seasoning.

Place noodles around the chicken and pour the sauce over all.

Moroccan Chicken Tagine with Soup Macaroni

Since *couscous,* the North African steamed grain dish, is one of my favorites, I particularly wanted some adaptation of it to noodles. The very fine acini de pepe, or "peppercorn" soup pasta, do very well in this dish—and, besides, are much simpler in preparation than *couscous,* which must be soaked, steamed, dried, and resteamed before eating.

1 chicken, cut into small serving pieces
4 cloves garlic, crushed
1 tablespoon coarse kosher salt
Juice of 2 limes
1 tablespoon ground ginger
1 teaspoon freshly ground black pepper
1 teaspoon hot paprika
1 teaspoon ground turmeric
¼ cup chopped chives
1 teaspoon ground cinnamon

¾ **cup chopped scallions**
3 **tablespoons margarine**
1 **large onion, thinly sliced**
½ **cup raisins**
1 **pound dried chick-peas, soaked overnight and**
cooked until tender, or 2 cans (20 ounces each)
chick-peas
1 **pound acini de pepe ("peppercorn" soup pasta)**
or large egg pastina
Harissa **(red pepper paste) optional**

Place the chicken pieces in a glass or ceramic bowl and toss with the garlic, salt, lime juice, ginger, and pepper. Refrigerate overnight.

Place the chicken and marinade in a heavy casserole. Add the paprika, turmeric, chives, cinnamon, and scallions to the casserole and add enough water to cover the chicken. Simmer for 1 hour, then remove the chicken pieces, set aside, and keep warm.

Continue to simmer the broth, while adding the margarine, onion, raisins, and chick-peas, until the sauce reduces somewhat and is thicker. Taste for seasoning, then add the chicken and heat through.

Meanwhile, boil the soup macaroni or pastina for about 8 minutes and drain well. In a large serving bowl mound the noodles and toss with a few spoons of sauce. Make a well in the center and spoon in the chicken and sauce. Serve with *harissa,* if desired.

Garlic Chicken in Noodles

Do not be distressed by the amount of garlic; when it stews for a long time, garlic loses its strength and becomes nutty rather than pungent. My guess is that the taste will no longer be definably "garlicky" to the uninitiated.

3 tablespoons olive oil
3 pounds chicken thighs and legs, in chunks, bones
and all
4 to 5 heads garlic, separated and peeled (see
note below)
2 bay leaves
1 tablespoon dried tarragon
½ cup chopped fresh parsley
½ teaspoon ground cinnamon
Salt and freshly ground black pepper to taste
1 cup dry white wine
1 pound egg noodles
½ cup buttered bread crumbs

Preheat the oven to 375 degrees.

Heat the oil in a heavy saucepan, then put in the chicken, along with the garlic, bay leaves, tarragon, parsley, cinnamon, salt, pepper, and wine. Cover tightly and simmer for 1 hour, stirring occasionally and adding a little water, if necessary.

Meanwhile, boil the egg noodles *al dente* (see page 24) and drain. Mix with the chicken and place in a buttered casserole. Top with the bread crumbs and bake for 30 minutes, or until the crumbs brown.

Note: If you place a garlic clove on a board and smack it with the side of a cleaver, it will loosen the skin. Or drop the cloves in boiling water for 10 seconds to loosen the skins.

Avgolemono Chicken with Noodles

Avgolemono sauce, the classic Greek egg-lemon sauce, is served with many dishes—from stuffed grape leaves to baked lamb with artichokes to broiled fish. Chicken and escarole are particularly good "bound" with *avgolemono*.

3 tablespoons butter
1 tablespoon vegetable oil
2 medium onions, chopped
½ cup chopped scallions
1 head escarole or chicory lettuce, cleaned and chopped
1 broiler chicken, in small chunks, bones and all
1 cup dry white wine
1 teaspoon dried tarragon
Salt and freshly ground black pepper to taste
1 pound egg noodles
4 egg yolks
¼ cup lemon juice
1 tablespoon grated lemon rind
1 teaspoon cornstarch mixed with 2 teaspoons cold water

In a heavy saucepan, heat the butter and oil over medium heat. Sauté the onions and scallions until brown, then add the lettuce and stir until wilted. Add the chicken and raise the heat a little, stirring as the pieces brown slightly. Add the wine, tarragon, salt, and pepper and cover the pan. Lower the heat to a simmer and cook for 20 minutes, then remove the chicken pieces.

Boil the noodles *al dente* (see page 24) and drain. Place in a warm serving dish.

Heat the chicken cooking liquid. Combine the remaining ingredients except the optional cornstarch mixture in a bowl and mix with a little of the hot liquid, whisking. Pour the contents of the bowl back into the saucepan and stir over very low heat as the sauce thickens. (If the sauce doesn't thicken enough, add the cornstarch mixture and stir over low heat.) Season with salt and pepper, then put the chicken on the bed of noodles and pour the sauce over all.

Poulet au Saffron

The combination of saffron and cinnamon is a key to the origin of this dish. It probably came to France from North Africa, via Spain.

1 chicken (3 pounds), cut in small serving pieces
1 tablespoon salt
½ teaspoon freshly ground black pepper
2 tablespoons butter
2 tablespoons olive oil
½ pound fresh mushrooms, sliced
10 small white onions, peeled
¼ teaspoon ground cinnamon
2 cloves garlic, minced
½ teaspoon dried thyme
½ cup dry white wine or vermouth
½ cup water
1 pound flat egg noodles
¼ teaspoon saffron
1 cup commercial sour cream (or crème fraîche
if you have it)

Rub the chicken with the salt and pepper. Heat the butter and oil in a heavy casserole, then brown the chicken pieces. Add the mushrooms, onions, and cinnamon and cook, stirring, over medium-high heat for 5 minutes. Add the garlic, thyme, wine, and water, then bring to a boil and simmer, covered, for 30 minutes, or until the chicken is tender but not falling from the bone.

Boil the egg noodles *al dente* (see page 24). Drain well and place in a large, deep serving bowl.

Combine the saffron and sour cream and stir into the chicken. Heat, but do not allow to boil.

Serve the chicken on top of the noodles.

Note: If you drop onions into boiling water for 10 seconds, the skins come off easily.

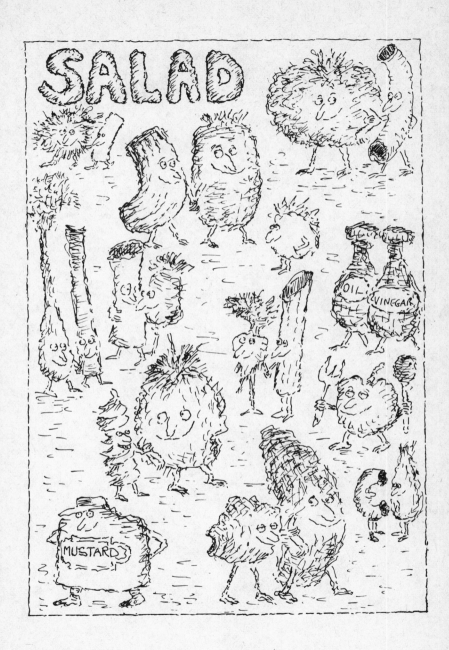

Salads and Side Dishes

Pasta and White Bean Salad

Like *pasta e fagioli,* this salad has good nutritional balance. It is also quite fresh tasting, with its variety of fresh herbs. With this dish, never be tempted to use canned beans.

½ pound dried white pea beans or haricot beans
½ pound small macaroni
1 clove garlic, finely minced
3 tablespoons minced fresh herbs (chives,
tarragon, parsley, etc.)
6 tablespoons olive oil
1 tablespoon wine vinegar
1 teaspoon dry mustard
Salt and freshly ground black pepper to taste
Pinch of granulated sugar

Soak the beans overnight, then boil until tender but not mushy. Drain and cool.

Boil the macaroni *al dente* (see page 24). Drain and cool under running water, then toss with the beans, garlic, and herbs. Chill.

Combine the oil, vinegar, mustard, salt, pepper, and sugar and pour over the salad. Toss and serve.

New Potato Salad with Pasta

New potatoes are a seasonal treat I look forward to each year. Don't try this salad without them.

3 medium new potatoes, scrubbed
1 cup small elbow macaroni
3 tablespoons chopped scallions
Salt and freshly ground black pepper to taste
¾ cup freshly made mayonnaise, thinned with a little lemon juice
Chopped fresh mint for garnish

Boil the potatoes until just tender. Skin while hot (cool just until you can touch them) and slice into a serving bowl.

Meanwhile, boil the pasta *al dente* (see page 24), drain well, and add to the bowl. Toss with the scallions, salt, pepper, and mayonnaise.

Chill until serving time, then garnish with mint and serve.

Fresh Blender Mayonnaise

1 large egg
½ teaspoon dry mustard
½ teaspoon salt
2 tablespoons lemon juice
1 cup olive oil

Break egg into blender. Add salt, mustard, and lemon juice, and ¼ cup of the oil. Cover and turn on, low speed. Uncover and add remaining oil in a slow stream, continuing to blend at low speed. It will be fairly thick. Makes about 1¼ cups.

Spiced Orzo Salad

Orzo is the very small, rice-shaped noodle that is a good rice substitute. This is a version, in fact, of my favorite rice salad.

1 ½ cups orzo (rice-shaped pasta)
1 tablespoon finely shredded fresh ginger *
Freshly ground black pepper
¼ cup chopped raisins (cut with a floured knife
to keep from sticking)
¼ cup chopped dried apricots
¼ cup olive oil
3 tablespoons lemon juice
3 scallions, chopped
2 tablespoons chopped fresh coriander or parsley

Boil the orzo *al dente* (see page 24), then drain and cool under running water. Place in a serving bowl and add the ginger, pepper, chopped raisins and apricots, olive oil, and lemon juice. Chill.

Just before serving, toss with the scallions and coriander or parsley.

Wianno Noodles

This is a chicken salad enlivened with fresh peppers and fresh herbs. Wianno is the Cape Cod home of Miss Ann Bird, where we first had this salad.

Salad

8 ounces elbow macaroni
½ pound cooked, cubed boneless chicken, tossed
with 2 tablespoons good mayonnaise
3 tablespoons chopped red onion
1 ½ green peppers, chopped
1 teaspoon granulated sugar
Salt and pepper to taste

Vinaigrette Dressing

3 tablespoons olive oil
1 tablespoon wine vinegar
2 cloves garlic, finely minced
¼ cup fresh dill or basil, finely chopped, or ½
teaspoon dried

Boil the noodles *al dente* (see page 24), then drain and cool under running water.

Combine the ingredients for the vinaigrette dressing, then toss the noodles in it. Add the chicken, onion, peppers, sugar, salt, and pepper. Mix well and serve immediately, or refrigerate to serve later. (This salad is better chilled.)

Herb Macaroni Salad

This recipe gives you a chance to choose your own flavorings. Several combinations are good—for instance, I like tarragon and chives. But fresh herbs only, please.

1 pound elbow or farfallette macaroni
3 tablespoons chopped fresh herbs (parsley, basil,
dill, tarragon, thyme, chives, fennel, sorrel,
savory, mint, etc.)
1 large sweet red pepper, seeded and sliced
Salt and freshly ground black pepper to taste
2 cups good mayonnaise, thinned slightly with
tarragon vinegar
4 hard-boiled eggs, sliced, for garnish
2 tablespoons chopped fresh parsley for garnish

Boil the macaroni *al dente* (see page 24), then drain and
cool under running water. Toss with the remaining ingredients, except for the garnishes, then place in a serving
dish and chill.

Serve, garnished with the sliced hard-boiled eggs and
parsley.

Avocado/Shrimp Noodles

An unusual version of shrimp salad that would be excellent
as an hors d'oeuvre or first course, along with a few rad-
ishes and black olives to garnish.

1 pound raw shrimps, peeled and deveined
1 cup water
2 ripe avocados, peeled and cut into 1-inch slices
Garlic Vinaigrette Dressing (page 269)
3 cups small elbow macaroni
3 tablespoons chopped parsley mixed with a little
fresh basil or thyme
Olive oil and lemon juice as needed

Boil the shrimps in the water for 3 minutes, then drain and
cool.

Marinate the avocado and shrimps in garlic vinaigrette
dressing for about 30 minutes.

Boil the elbow macaroni *al dente* (see page 24), then
drain and cool under running water. Toss the macaroni with
the shrimp and avocado mixture, then top with the chopped
parsley mixture. Add olive oil and lemon juice to taste and
serve.

Indian Salad

Cooked pork, marinated in a sharp vinaigrette and then
combined with macaroni tossed in curried mayonnaise, is
a good luncheon dish. You might also use cold chicken,
turkey, shrimp, or veal. And, if you prefer, romaine lettuce
leaves may be used as a base for the salad.

Vinaigrette Dressing

¼ cup olive oil
2 tablespoons white wine vinegar
2 tablespoons minced chives
1 teaspoon dry mustard
Salt and freshly ground black pepper to taste

Salad

1 pound lean cooked pork, in shreds
2 cucumbers, peeled, cut lengthwise, seeded, and
julienned
1 tablespoon coarse salt
2 cups macaroni, cooked *al dente* (see page 24),
drained, and chilled
½ cup freshly made mayonnaise
2 teaspoons imported curry powder, preferably
Madras *
Chopped scallions or fresh coriander for garnish

Mix the dressing ingredients and marinate the pork in them for 1 hour.

Combine the cucumber with the coarse salt and set aside for 30 minutes. Drain and pat dry, then combine with the pork, macaroni, and mayonnaise, which has been mixed with the curry powder.

Mound the salad, garnish with the scallions or coriander, and serve.

Chicken Salad with Grapes

An interesting "Roquefort" style dressing for chicken, nuts, grapes, and noodles. Toss it all together just at the last minute.

Salad

12 ounces egg noodles
3 large whole chicken breasts, roasted or
simmered in broth or water until firm
3 ounces sliced almonds, toasted in 1 tablespoon
butter until golden (do not let burn)
1 pound seedless green grapes, washed and stems
removed
2 scallions, chopped
2 tablespoons blue cheese, crumbled

Dressing

¼ pound blue cheese
2 tablespoons lemon juice, or more to taste
¼ cup olive oil or mayonnaise
Salt and freshly ground black pepper to taste
1 tablespoon fresh dill or 1 teaspoon dried dill
weed

Boil the noodles *al dente* (see page 24), then drain, run under cold water, and chill.

Shred the chicken into 1-inch strips, then combine with the almonds, grapes, scallions, and crumbled blue cheese.

Place all the dressing ingredients in the blender and blend until smooth.

Place the noodles and chicken mixture in a serving bowl and top with the dressing. Toss well and serve.

Mauna Loa Seafood Salad

This luscious mixture of exotic tastes is an invention of my friend Andrea Bell. Tossed with cold penne or cut macaroni, it is a main-course salad.

Dressing

1 shallot, finely minced
1 clove garlic, finely minced
1½ cups good mayonnaise
3 tablespoons chili sauce
2 scallions, both green part and white, finely chopped
1 teaspoon Worcestershire sauce
¼ teaspoon Tabasco
½ teaspoon dry mustard

Salad

1 pound large shrimps, peeled, deveined, and cooked
1 pound cooked crab, shredded
2 avocados, peeled and sliced
2 cans (11 ounces each) mandarin oranges, drained
1 pound penne or cut macaroni, boiled *al dente* (see page 24), then drained and cooled under running water
1 small jar macadamia nuts, roughly cracked
1 small can pecans, roughly cracked

Mix all dressing ingredients together. Toss with the shrimps, crab, avocados, mandarin oranges, and noodles, then chill for 2 hours. Just before serving, toss with the macadamia nuts and pecans.

Bean Sprout Salad with Noodles

A very good salad to accompany grilled food, like chicken *yakitori* or broiled fish. Use only fresh bean sprouts (easily grown in your kitchen)—canned sprouts are soggy and have a poor flavor.

6 ounces bean thread noodles *
3 ounces fresh bean sprouts
3 scallions, chopped
2 tablespoons dried shrimp, * **which has been**
soaked in warm water for 15 minutes (optional)
2 tablespoons rice wine vinegar *
2 tablespoons soy sauce *
1 teaspoon granulated sugar
1 teaspoon sesame oil *
Salt and freshly ground black pepper to taste

Soak the bean thread noodles in hot water for 10 minutes, then drain and place under running water to cool.

Wash the bean sprouts, then drain. Toss with the cooled noodles, scallions, and dried shrimp.

Combine the remaining ingredients, toss with the bean sprout mixture, and serve.

Small Bows with Beans and Tuna

A very nice appetizer or part of an antipasto. You can give this salad an interesting "bite" by stirring a small amount of *harissa*, a red pepper paste from North Africa, into the dressing, thus making it resemble the Tunisian salad called *méchouia*.

1 cup small pasta bows (farfalle or farfallette)
1 purple onion, thinly sliced
1 cup small white beans, soaked overnight and
boiled until tender *but not mushy* (2 or 3 hours
for old beans)
Salt and freshly ground black pepper to taste
Garlic Vinaigrette Dressing (page 269)
1 can (6 ounces) tuna, drained and separated into
rough chunks
1 sweet red pepper, seeded and sliced into very
thin strands

Boil the pasta *al dente* (see page 24). Drain and cool under running water, then toss with the onions, beans, salt, pepper, and dressing. Mound the tuna on top, decorate with strands of red pepper, and serve.

Antipasto Noodles

This is a kind of one-pot antipasto in which pasta serves as a base for contrasting tastes, such as spicy sausage, tangy cheese, and sardines. You could add olives, marinated mushrooms, or any other cold salad ingredient.

1 pound noodles
1 cup farmers or feta cheese
2 ounces peperoni slices, chopped
½ cucumber, peeled and sliced
2 hard-boiled eggs
1 can (4 ounces) sardines
Salt and freshly ground pepper to taste
Garlic Vinaigrette Dressing (page 269)

Cook the noodles *al dente* (see page 24). Drain and run under cold water.

Mix the cheese and peperoni into the noodles, then lay slices of cucumber, hard-boiled eggs, and sardines on top of the mixture. Season with salt and pepper, top with the dressing and serve.

Tossed Salad with Garlic Noodles

Noodles here are like garlic croutons for salad; they are deep-fried after being marinated with garlic. This garnish can be used for other dishes—for topping gratinées, and so forth.

Salad

2 cups corn oil
**1 cup thin spaghetti, broken into 2-inch strips and
cooked** *al dente* **(see page 24)**
½ head romaine lettuce
**Equal amount of carefully washed fresh spinach
leaves, tough stems removed**
1 cup cherry tomatoes, sliced across
3 scallions, chopped
3 cloves garlic, mashed well
3 tablespoons salad oil

Garlic Lemon Dressing

1 teaspoon dry mustard
1 tablespoon water
1 clove garlic, finely chopped
1 teaspoon granulated sugar
1 teaspoon salt
1 cup olive oil
3 tablespoons lemon juice
1 teaspoon grated onion (optional)

Heat the corn oil in a deep saucepan or deep-fryer to 400
degrees on a deep-frying thermometer. Spread the pasta on
paper towels and fry, a small amount at a time, until
golden brown and crisp. Remove with a slotted spoon and
drain on paper towels.

Combine the remaining salad ingredients, then sprinkle
with noodles just before tossing with the garlic lemon
dressing.

Alsatian Noodles

The simplest noodle side dish. Wonderful when made with
fresh noodles, as an accompaniment to broiled dishes.

1 pound egg noodles
1½ cups toasted bread crumbs
⅜ pound (1½ sticks) butter, in small pieces
Salt and freshly ground pepper to taste

Boil the noodles *al dente* (see page 24). Drain and place in a serving dish, then toss with the bread crumbs, butter, and salt and pepper.

Cold Noodles with Tahini Dressing

Tahini is ground sesame seeds, a wonderful ingredient to know. If you haven't a Middle Eastern supplier, you can grind the seed in a blender to produce *tahini*. This sauce is also good with cooked vegetables, especially eggplant.

1 pound vermicelli
3 tablespoons *tahini*
2 cloves garlic, finely minced
2 tablespoons lemon juice
Salt and freshly ground pepper to taste
1 tablespoon water
½ to ¾ cup olive oil

Place the *tahini* is a small bowl and mix in the garlic, lemon juice, salt, pepper, and water. Blend until smooth.

Gradually add the olive oil, while whisking with fork until smooth and medium thick (as in making mayonnaise).

Boil the vermicelli *al dente* (see page 24), then drain, cool under running water, and toss with the sauce.

DESSERTS

Desserts, Near Noodles, and Miscellany

DESSERTS

The following is a series of "noodle puddings" culled from several traditions. These are all sweet, but, surprisingly, not always intended as desserts. I am grateful to Eleanor Wurgaft for her suggestions.

Noodle Kugel

1 pound broad egg noodles, boiled *al dente* (see page 24) and drained
1 pound cottage cheese
3 eggs
¼ cup granulated sugar
½ teaspoon ground cinnamon
1 teaspoon vanilla extract
¼ cup melted butter
1 cup milk
Raisins and nuts to taste
1 cup crushed cornflakes

Preheat the oven to 350 degrees.

Combine all the ingredients except the cornflakes; add the eggs, beaten, last. Butter a 9 × 13-inch roasting pan or casserole and add the mixture. Top with the crushed cornflakes and bake for 35 minutes.

Noodle Pudding Soufflé

8 eggs, separated
1 pint commercial sour cream
8 ounces cottage cheese
2 cups milk
¾ cup granulated sugar
1 teaspoon vanilla extract
2 cups fine egg noodles, boiled *al dente* (see
page 24) and drained
Grated rind of 1 lemon
¼ pound (1 stick) butter
1 can (16 ounces) pitted dark cherries, drained
½ teaspoon ground cinnamon

Preheat the oven to 350 degrees.

Combine the egg yolks, sour cream, cottage cheese, milk, sugar, and vanilla in the blender and blend until smooth.

Place the noodles in a mixing bowl and add the blended mixture and the grated lemon rind.

Beat the egg whites until stiff.

Melt the butter in a heavy casserole. Fold the egg whites into the noodle mixture and place in the casserole. Bake for 1 hour, or until puffed and brown, then remove from the oven and cool to warm. (Or let cool and reheat for 10 minutes at 350 degrees.) Surround with the cherries, sprinkle with the cinnamon, and serve.

Noodle Pudding with Apricots

½ cup granulated sugar
2 eggs, separated
1 teaspoon ground cinnamon

2 tablespoons butter
½ pound broad egg noodles, cooked *al dente* (see page 24) and drained
1 can (11 ounces) apricot halves
1 can (8 ounces) pineapple tidbits

Preheat the oven to 325 degrees.

Combine the sugar and egg yolks and beat well. Add the cinnamon and melted butter. Beat the egg whites until stiff and fold in, together with the drained noodles.

Grease a casserole. Put in half of the noodle mixture. Drain apricot halves and pineapple tidbits. Add half the fruits to the noodle mixture, and then the reserved half of the noodles, top with remaining fruits, and bake for 30 minutes, then serve.

Noodle Dairy Pudding

10 ounces medium egg noodles
½ teaspoon ground cinnamon
Salt to taste
½ cup raisins
½ cup granulated sugar
1 teaspoon almond extract
2 cups milk
3 eggs
¼ pound (1 stick) butter

Preheat the oven to 350 degrees.

Boil the noodles *al dente* (see page 24), then drain and run cold water through them. Place in a mixing bowl and add the cinnamon, salt, raisins, sugar, and almond extract.

Beat the milk and eggs together and add to the noodle mixture, then melt half of the butter and add this to the mixture.

Heat the remaining butter in a baking dish, then pour in the noodle mixture and bake until the pudding is well browned, about 50 minutes.

Hungarian Baked Noodle Dessert

Hungarian noodle desserts are related to Jewish noodle puddings, but are more definitely desserts, and usually do not appear earlier in the meal, as do Jewish noodle puddings.

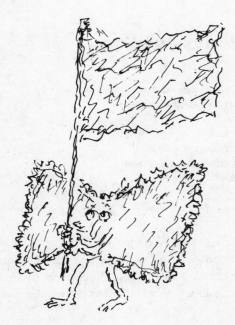

8 ounces wide noodles
3 tablespoons butter
½ cup chopped walnuts
3 tablespoons apricot jam
Grated rind of 1 lemon
2 tablespoons bread crumbs
1 cup sour cream
⅓ cup granulated sugar
Confectioner's sugar

Preheat the oven to 350 degrees.

Boil the noodles *al dente* (see page 24), then drain well. Combine while warm with the butter, nuts, jam, lemon rind, bread crumbs and granulated sugar. Stir in the sour cream, then place in a greased baking dish and bake for 30 minutes.

Dust with confectioner's sugar and serve.

Hawaiian Banana Pudding with Vermicelli

A dessert so sweet and rich your teeth will sing. Make small portions.

4 bananas
2 cups coconut milk (see page 41) (or use canned coconut milk and leave out the honey)
¼ cup honey
2 tablespoons cornstarch
½ cup water
1 teaspoon lemon juice
2 cups broken-up vermicelli, boiled *al dente* (see page 24) and drained
Canned coconut cream and/or coconut flakes

Cook the bananas in the coconut milk for 15 minutes. Add the honey, then put through a sieve.

Mix the cornstarch, water, and lemon juice and add to the banana mixture. Cook, stirring, as the mixture thickens, then remove from the heat and stir in the vermicelli. Chill in individual cups, then serve with coconut cream and/or garnish with coconut flakes.

Pasta Dolce

A very sweet and heavy pudding that reminds me a little of English nursery puddings. Try serving it with heavy cream.

**½ pound small macaroni or acini de pepe
("peppercorn" soup pasta)
3 cups milk
¼ cup granulated sugar
¼ cup brown sugar
¼ teaspoon freshly grated nutmeg
½ teaspoon ground cinnamon
Chopped walnuts for garnish**

Boil the macaroni in the milk (being careful not to let it boil over) for 8 minutes. Add the sugars and cook for 10 more minutes, stirring. Add the nutmeg and cinnamon and serve lukewarm or hot, garnished with the chopped walnuts.

Phaluda (Cornstarch Vermicelli)

These noodles are very unusual; a pale bluish white, they are not cooked in the ordinary way at all, but are merely a cornstarch paste "hardened" in cold water. I had them first in Delhi, as a bed for the remarkable rosewater frozen cream *kulfi*.

**¾ cup cornstarch mixed with
1½ cups water**

Stir over medium heat for about 12 minutes as the mixture changes from watery to very thick, then translucent bluish, then loosens up just a bit.

Have ready a bowl of ice water and a spaetzle maker or a potato ricer. But a spoonful of pasta through the press over the water and let the noodles fall into the water directly as you press them. They will firm slightly into thin, translucent vermicelli bits. Keep in the water until needed, then drain and serve under almond syrup and softened vanilla ice cream, or either of the following:

Kulfi

**1 can (13 ounces) sweetened condensed milk
1 cup heavy cream
1½ teaspoons rosewater or vanilla extract
¼ cup almonds, finely chopped (not ground in the
blender)
¼ cup pistachio nuts, finely chopped
½ cup granulated sugar
6 tablespoons water**

Combine the condensed milk, ½ teaspoon of the rosewater or vanilla extract, and the nuts. Stir well and freeze. During the freezing, which takes 4 hours or more, the nuts rise to the top. Serve with a mixture of the sugar and water boiled for 5 minutes. Then add the remaining teaspoon rosewater and chill.

Fruits in Syrup

**1 can (11 ounces) mandarin oranges, 2
tablespoons of the syrup reserved
1 can (8 ounces) cubed pineapple
1 small can lichees
2 bananas, sliced
1 teaspoon lemon juice
2 tablespoons honey**

Combine all the ingredients and chill.

NEAR NOODLES

Many of the recipes given in this book would be delicious with these "not-quite" noodles instead of *pasta secca* or freshly made noodles, and many of the sauces are excellent with them.

The sorts of crêpes given are not the classic French sort (for which you can find recipes elsewhere), but a Korean pancake, which is served rolled with spiced beef shreds, scallion, cooked egg strips, and chilies; a manicotti crêpe that is rolled with various stuffings and baked with tomato sauce; and blintzes, for cheese and meat fillings.

The other kinds of "near noodles" are Italian gnocchi, German or Czech spaetzle, and Hungarian *csipetke,* all of which could also be called "near dumplings." They are kinds of dumplings to be boiled in water before serving with sauces and meats, or gratinéed with butter and cheese.

Blintzes

These "crêpes" are, of course, most often served with a cheese filling, and with a big spoonful of sour cream on the top. You could also use a ground meat filling, or a fruit filling.

2 eggs
1 cup all-purpose flour
1 tablespoon peanut oil
1 ½ cups milk
Cheese Filling for Blintzes or Kreplach (see below)
Butter for frying
Sour cream

Beat the eggs until light, then add the flour and oil and mix until smooth. Add the milk, stirring until the butter is smooth and thin.

Heat a small (6- to 8-inch) skillet and grease lightly with more oil. Pour a small ladleful (about 2 tablespoons) of batter in, tilting the pan so the batter covers the bottom. Cook until the bottom is browned, then turn carefully to brown the other side. Stack the pancakes on a plate or towel as they are finished.

Prepare the cheese filling as directed below.

To fill the blintzes, place a heaping teaspoonful of filling in the center of each pancake. Roll the pancake up loosely, then, with the seam on the bottom, tuck the ends in.

Heat enough butter in a skillet to coat the bottom generously, then fry the blintzes, a few at a time, first on the seam side until golden brown, then on the top.

Serve immediately, topped with a spoonful of sour cream.

Cheese Filling for Blintzes or Kreplach

1 ¼ pounds dry cottage cheese, or pot cheese, or ricotta
2 eggs
Salt and freshly ground black pepper to taste
2 tablespoons melted butter

Combine all the ingredients and mix well until smooth.
Use in blintzes (see above) or kreplach.

Hungarian Csipetke

These are closest to spaetzle, but, because they are made by pinching the dough with the fingers, they are usually called "pinched noodles."

1 cup all-purpose flour
Salt
1 egg
Butter or oil

Place the flour and ½ teaspoon salt in a bowl and make a well in the center. Add the egg to the well, then enough water to make a soft dough. Knead until smooth.

Bring a kettle of water to boiling. Add salt to taste.

Roll out the dough to about ⅛ inch thick. Pinch off pieces about ½ inch in size and drop them into the boiling water. When they rise to the surface, they are done. Drain well and toss with butter or oil before serving.

Note: These are also good added to a soup after they have been boiled.

Korean Pancakes

These are similar to crêpes, but are eaten with an interesting meal of lightly sautéed beef strips, shredded vegetables, scallions, and a sauce of sesame seeds, garlic, soy sauce, and chopped ginger. Or are a delicious substitute for the much more difficult *moo shi* pancakes served with "mandarin" style dishes.

1½ cups all-purpose flour
2 eggs, lightly beaten
2 cups milk
6 tablespoons melted butter

Place the flour in bowl. Beat together the remaining ingredients and add to the flour, stirring with a whisk.

Brush a 6-inch pan with butter or tasteless oil. Heat the pan and add a small ladleful of batter (about 2 tablespoons), swirling the pan so the batter covers the bottom. Cook until the crêpe is set, then cook briefly on the other side. Stack the pancakes as they are done.

These can be set aside for an hour or so, and used at room temperature.

Manicotti Crêpes

1 cup all-purpose flour
¾ cup plus 2 tablespoons milk
6 eggs
Salt to taste

Place the flour in mixing bowl. Add the milk a little at a time, while beating with a wire whisk, then add the eggs, one at a time, beating well after every addition. Add salt to taste, and strain the batter well. The batter can be set aside or refrigerated for an hour or so.

Brush a 6-inch pan with olive oil or butter. Heat the pan, then add batter, one ladleful (about 2 tablespoons) for each crêpe, and swirl the pan around so the batter covers the bottom. Cook just until the crêpe is set, then turn and cook very briefly on the other side.

Turn the crêpe out onto waxed paper, and, as each crêpe is made, turn it onto the pile, separating each with waxed paper. Use immediately, stuffed with one of the fillings on pages 270–277, or store in the refrigerator until needed. After stuffing and rolling, the crêpes can be baked with a sauce, or gratinéed with cheese under a broiler.

Note: Any leftover crêpes can be saved, cut in strips and used in soups. They are very good in escarole soup with grated Parmesan.

Spaetzle

The first time I ever had this was in the kitchen of a German friend, who had just completed weeks of marinating beef, searing it on a grill three floors down, and slow cooking it into the most marvelous sauerbraten I've ever had. The spaetzle were made over a huge kettle of boiling water, in a contraption, looking like a ricer, made just for these light, eggy dumpling strands.

Spaetzle are wonderful with much less troublesome foods than sauerbraten; however—tomato sauces, chicken livers in sour cream, a light vegetable sauce. And by themselves, drained, tossed with butter and cheese and put under the broiler for a couple of minutes, they are fine.

4 cups all-purpose flour
4 eggs
3 tablespoons cream
Salt and freshly ground pepper to taste
Pinch of freshly grated nutmeg
2 tablespoons melted butter

Combine all the ingredients except the melted butter in a mixing bowl and beat well. Force through a spaetzle maker, ricer, or colander—or spread out on floured board and simply cut off ribbons of the mixture—into a kettle of boiling, salted water. Poach for 5 minutes, then remove with a slotted spoon to a colander and drain for a minute or so. Place in a serving dish and toss with melted butter.

Potato Gnocchi

For a long time, I made these with only one sauce, a chicken livers in wine sauce, only recently to discover how good they are with many other sauces, even plain tomato sauce. They are very easy to make.

2 pounds potatoes, peeled and quartered
2 cups all-purpose flour
2 eggs
2 tablespoons butter, melted
½ teaspoon salt

Boil the potatoes until tender, then drain and mash or put through a ricer into a mixing bowl. Add the flour, eggs, and butter and season with salt. Knead until smooth (the dough should be fairly soft).

Have a kettle of water boiling. With a teaspoon, scoop up ½ teaspoonfuls of the dough at a time, releasing it from the spoon with another teaspoon and dropping it into the water. Let the gnocchi boil for about three minutes; they should float to the surface.

Remove the gnocchi with a slotted spoon and let them drain, then place them in a serving dish and toss with sauce, or with butter and cheese. They can be run under the broiler with cheese, to brown. Good also with a pesto sauce (see pages 266–267 or page 71).

Semolina Gnocchi

These are made in a different way from the potato gnocchi —instead of being boiled, these are cut out of a firm dough and broiled or heated with their sauce.

1 ¼ cups milk
4 to 6 ounces semolina or Cream of Wheat
Salt and freshly ground black pepper to taste
Pinch of freshly grated nutmeg
3 ounces freshly grated Parmesan cheese
2 eggs

Bring the milk to a boil and stir in the semolina, salt, pepper, and nutmeg. Stir over heat until the mixture is *very* thick, then remove from the heat and stir in the cheese. Beat in the eggs, one at a time.

Butter a baking sheet and pour the mixture onto it to a depth of about ¼ inch. Chill, then cut the dough into rounds or cut into small squares and place them in a greased gratin dish. Heat for 20 minutes in a 325-degree oven with sauce or cheese.

Indian Chick-pea Noodle Snack

Similar deep-fried snacks are sold everywhere in India—
often brightly colored, sometimes glistening with syrup.

½ pound chick-pea flour *
1 teaspoon or more imported curry powder,
preferably Madras *
Salt
Plain yogurt as needed
Corn oil for deep frying

Combine the flour, curry powder, and 1 teaspoon salt.
Add just enough yogurt to make a paste; it should not be
at all runny.

Heat oil in a deep saucepan to 350 degrees on a deep-
frying thermometer. Uusing a potato ricer or spaetzle
maker, force the mixture through into the hot oil, a little
at a time, to make thin "noodle shreds." Fry until the
noodles are golden and crisp.

Remove with a slotted spoon onto paper towels to
drain. Toss with salt and serve as a cocktail snack.

SAUCES

Although directions for most sauces are contained in the recipes, some reappear so often or are so basic or interesting that I include them here for reference. This will also allow you to experiment with them, to use them in contexts different from the ones you'll find in this book.

Fresh Tomato Sauce

2 tablespoons olive oil
1 onion, finely chopped
1 clove garlic, finely minced
2 pounds fresh tomatoes, peeled, seeded, and chopped (see note, page 51)
½ teaspoon dried thyme
1 tablespoon fresh basil or 1 teaspoon dried
Salt and freshly ground black pepper to taste
Pinch of granulated sugar

Heat the olive oil in a heavy saucepan. Sauté the onion and garlic until golden, then add the tomatoes. Add the herbs and other seasonings and let simmer until the tomatoes are soft and are turning into a puree.

Put through a food mill or sieve, then back into the pan for further cooking if not thick enough.

Lew's Spaghetti Sauce

2 tablespoons olive oil
1 medium onion, chopped
¾ pound ground beef

1 can (35 ounces) Italian tomatoes
1 can (6 ounces) tomato paste
1 green pepper, finely chopped (optional)
½ pound fresh mushrooms, chopped
¼ cup fresh basil or 2 tablespoons dried
1 tablespoon granulated sugar
Salt and freshly ground black pepper to taste

Heat the olive oil in a heavy saucepan and sauté the onion until soft. Add the meat and brown it, stirring to separate, then add the tomatoes and tomato paste, crushing the tomatoes with a wooden spoon until soft.

Add the green pepper, mushrooms, and seasonings and stir the sauce until the ingredients are thoroughly mixed. Simmer for 30 minutes before serving.

Note: This sauce improves on keeping.

Tomato Paste Sauce

½ cup chopped onion
¼ cup olive oil
2 cans (6 ounces each) tomato paste
2¼ cups water
¼ teaspoon salt
2 cloves garlic, finely minced
Freshly ground black pepper to taste
½ teaspoon granulated sugar
½ teaspoon dried oregano
1 bay leaf

Sauté the onion in the olive oil until golden. Add the tomato paste, then slowly add the water to the mixture, stirring constantly. Add the remaining ingredients and simmer for 30 minutes, stirring occasionally. Remove the bay leaf before serving.

Walnut Pesto Sauce I

This is a nice variation on the basic basil pesto. For the best pesto of the basil sort, see the recipe for Frank Phillips' Pesto, page 71.

¼ cup pignoli (pine nuts)
½ cup chopped walnuts
2 teaspoons finely chopped fresh basil
½ cup olive oil
Salt and freshly ground black pepper to taste
½ cup freshly grated Parmesan cheese

Place the pignoli, walnuts, and basil in the blender (or in a mortar) and blend or mash well. Gradually add the olive oil, blending or mashing as you do. Add salt and pepper and the Parmesan and mix well. Toss with pasta just before serving.

Walnut Pesto Sauce II

½ cup ground walnuts
¾ cup chopped fresh parsley
2 tablespoons softened butter
3 tablespoons fine bread crumbs
½ cup olive oil
2 tablespoons heavy cream
Salt and freshly ground black pepper to taste

Place the walnuts and parsley in a mortar or small bowl. Add the softened butter and mash into a paste. Add the bread crumbs and then the oil, a little at a time, and blend until the mixture is smooth. Add the cream and salt and pepper.

Dill Pesto

½ cup olive oil
4 cloves garlic, minced
1 ½ cup roughly chopped fresh dill
Salt and freshly ground black pepper to taste
½ cup freshly grated Parmesan cheese

Combine all the ingredients except the Parmesan in the blender and blend well. Stir in the Parmesan and serve.

White Sauce (Bechamel, Besciamella)

2 tablespoons butter
2 tablespoons all-purpose flour
2 cups milk, scalded
¼ cup heavy cream
3 egg yolks
Salt and white pepper to taste
Pinch of freshly grated nutmeg

Melt the butter in a heavy saucepan. Over low heat, stir in the flour; continue to stir for 2 or 3 minutes. Add the milk, while you stir the mixture with a wire whisk, and simmer for 10 minutes.

Beat the cream and egg yolks together and add a little hot sauce to the mixture, whisking continually. Add the yolk mixture back to the saucepan and heat without boiling. Remove from the heat and season to taste.

Cold Sesame Sauce for Noodles

1 tablespoon sesame oil *
2 teaspoons rice wine vinegar *
2 tablespoons soy sauce *
2 scallions, finely chopped
1 teaspoon granulated sugar
2 teaspoons sesame seeds, toasted in a heavy
skillet until golden

Combine all the ingredients and beat to dissolve the sugar.
Toss with bean thread or other Oriental noodles.

Oyster Sauce for Noodles

1 teaspoon sesame oil *
2 cloves garlic, mashed
1 tablespoon rice wine vinegar *
½ teaspoon salt
3 tablespoons oyster sauce *
1 tablespoon soy sauce *

Combine all ingredients and heat slightly. Toss with
cooked meats, vegetables, or hot, drained noodles.

Spicy Noodle Dipping Sauce
(for Chinese or Korean Noodles)

1 teaspoon chili paste with garlic *
2 tablespoons rice wine vinegar *

2 tablespoons soy sauce *
1 teaspoon granulated sugar
1 teaspoon sesame oil *

Combine all the ingredients and serve as a dipping sauce for cooked vegetables, meats, or noodles.

Garlic Vinaigrette Dressing

1 teaspoon dry mustard
1 tablespoon water
1 clove garlic, finely minced
1 teaspoon granulated sugar
1 teaspoon salt
1 cup olive oil
3 tablespoons lemon juice or wine vinegar
1 teaspoon freshly grated onion (optional)

Combine the mustard with the water and let stand for 10 minutes, then add the garlic, sugar, salt, and olive oil and let stand for 1 hour.

Add the lemon juice or vinegar and the onion, then pour into a screw-top jar and shake well.

Savory Butters for Noodles

These butters can be made ahead and packed in refrigerator containers, or frozen for use with hot breads as well as with noodles. However, garlic butter should only be frozen, as it can turn rancid in the refrigerator after a day or two.

For each 2 ounces of butter add:
1 teaspoon fresh herbs; or ½ clove garlic, crushed;
or 1 tablespoon parsley, finely chopped; or 1
teaspoon anchovy paste

Let the butter soften, then add your choice of herb or flavoring and blend well.

Toss 1 pound of pasta with 2 or 3 tablespoons of flavored butter.

STUFFINGS

The following are recipes for stuffings or fillings for pasta —the large shells, the tubes, the rolled cannelloni and manicotti, lasagne and tortellini.

Beef-Spinach Stuffing

¾ cup very finely minced cold, cooked beef
2 cups finely chopped cooked spinach
3 scallions, very finely chopped
1 egg
Salt and freshly ground black pepper to taste

Combine all the ingredients and beat well.

Veal and Pork Stuffing

2 small onions, finely minced
2 tablespoons butter

1 cup ground veal
½ cup ground pork
1 egg
1 clove garlic, mashed
Salt and freshly ground black pepper to taste
¼ cup freshly grated Parmesan cheese

Heat the butter in a skillet until melted, then add the
onions and sauté until golden. Scrape into a mixing bowl
and combine with all the remaining ingredients. (Caution: Since this filling contains pork, be sure that the finished dish is cooked through—and if you wish to taste the
mixture for seasoning before stuffing your pasta, do so by
sautéing a small amount in butter.)

Ricotta-Spinach Filling

3 tablespoons butter or margarine
3 medium onions, finely chopped
1 package (10 ounces) fresh spinach, washed
and picked over
2 cups ricotta cheese
1 egg
½ cup freshly grated Parmesan cheese
Pinch of freshly grated nutmeg
Salt and freshly ground black pepper to taste

Heat the butter in a heavy skillet and sauté the onions until
golden. Add the spinach, cover, and cook until the spinach
is wilted. Remove from the heat and chop finely, then add
remaining ingredients and beat well.

Hungarian Sweet Filling for Pasta

This, in a sort of ravioli that is dusted with sugar after boiling, makes a very interesting dessert.

2 tablespoons semolina or Cream of Wheat
1 cup milk
⅓ cup granulated sugar
1 to 2 cups sour cream
1 egg
1 tablespoon grated lemon rind

In a small saucepan, heat the milk to simmering and cook the semolina in it for 5 minutes. Off the heat, beat in the remaining ingredients. Use in tortellini-like forms or in ravioli. Boil, drain, and serve sprinkled with sugar.

Index